D1523498

what matters?

Chapters by

Joan Gillette

Rebecca Huntsman

Noel K. Jones

Donna B. Lindquist

Diane Stephens

Jennifer Story

Janine Toomes

what matters?

A PRIMER FOR TEACHING READING

Edited by Diane Stephens

Center for the Study of Reading, University of Illinois at Urbana-Champaign

HEINEMANN
PORTSMOUTH, NH

contents

Preface   ix

It Matters That Teachers Understand How Language Is Learned
Chapter One
OBSERVING LEARNERS: WHAT THEY KNOW
ABOUT LANGUAGE   Janine Toomes   3

It Matters That Teachers Understand That Reading Is Strategic
Chapter Two
INVITING THE LITERACY LEARNER TO ENGAGE
IN READING   Donna B. Lindquist   15

It Matters That Teachers Make Informed Observations
Chapter Three
BUILDING ON WHAT MATTERS   Janine Toomes,
Diane Stephens, and Joan Gillette   23

It Matters That Teachers Use Response to Support Learning
Chapter Four
QUESTIONING AND RESPONDING   Rebecca Huntsman   37

It Matters That Teachers Establish Learning-Centered Environments
Chapter Five
GETTING STARTED: CREATING A LITERATE CLASSROOM
ENVIRONMENT   Noel K. Jones   49

It Matters That Teachers Continually Reflect
Chapter Six
TOUCHSTONES FOR TEACHING   Jennifer Story   63

Afterword   71

Works Cited   73

preface

"Jigarees here, jigarees there,
jigarees jump everywhere . . . "

Five of us—four teachers finishing a master's degree in reading education and I, their professor—were watching a videotape (Wright Group 1987) of a shared reading lesson (Holdaway 1979). We didn't know the teacher on the videotape, a Mrs. O'Brian, but we all wished we did. She was quite impressive. We'd recently been talking about response as a teaching strategy and we were watching Mrs. O'Brian closely, trying to write down everything she did that made her seem effective at teaching through response. We had to pause the machine in order to keep up.

Earlier that week, I'd shown the same videotape to my undergraduate class of college juniors taking their first reading course. They too saw Mrs. O'Brian introduce and carry out a shared reading lesson. I asked them to take notes during the tape and told them that we would discuss afterwards the strategies that Mrs. O'Brian used to help her "first-year" children in New Zealand learn to read. Brenda opened the discussion by commenting, "I don't understand how she gets them to stand up, act out a part of a book, and then sit back down again so quietly." Bob continued, "Yeah, she has done a really good job controlling them." Sandy added, "I wonder how long it took her to teach the children the rules for how to behave?"

I expected there to be a difference of course. In terms of what they know about reading, teaching, and learning, undergraduates just beginning education courses are worlds apart from experienced teachers finishing a master's degree in reading. But I found myself wondering how to help the undergraduates appreciate the things on the tape that the graduate students and I thought really mattered. Mrs. O'Brian used response to teach and she was a master of that art, but the undergraduates hadn't heard her teaching through conversation. How could I help them see the artfulness of the teacher? How could I help them focus on what the teacher was helping the children learn about language and books? After all, in what looked like and sounded like conversation, the teacher had managed to communicate that:

- A book has a beginning, middle, and end.
- The text itself has a front and a back.
- Print is read from left to right and top to bottom.
- Size of print and punctuation give clues to intonation.
- Books tell a story.

- Pictures are useful in making predictions.
- Predictions are helpful whether or not they're accurate.
- Reading is fun and exciting, a treat to look forward to.
- Reading is a social process.
- You learn new things from reading.
- Children already know a lot.
- Students in the class could read and were good readers.
- Good readers made predictions and connections.

And that was just a partial list!

I brought my concerns to the graduate seminar and found the teachers had similar concerns. As graduate assistants, they supervised student teachers and wanted to know how to help pre-service teachers develop a framework for examining what they were doing and seeing. As parents of young children, they wondered how to share their new insights and understanding with their children's teachers.

We all wanted to share our understandings about reading, but had no simple means of doing so. How to share? What to share? We couldn't hand people a pile of the books and articles we'd read over the last two years and expect them to scurry over to some quiet corner and begin to read. After all, we'd read at least twelve of the same books, probably a hundred of the same articles, and had shared with each other numerous other books and articles. Even if anyone responded enthusiastically to our pile of recommended readings, it wouldn't answer the immediate need. We wanted *this semester's* student teachers to understand the importance of asking real questions instead of reading preformed questions out of the teachers' manual. We wanted classroom teachers to help the children feel good about themselves as readers and encourage them to take risks as readers *this year*. We wanted undergraduates *currently enrolled* in methods classes to be really "seeing" during their field experiences and just not "recording" information about the cuteness of bulletin boards or the neatness of lesson plans. Where should we begin? How best to share what we knew?

We began to think about writing a short paper for interested pre- and in-service teachers. At first we thought we should write something on response. Then we took a step back and realized that in order for teachers to use response effectively as a method, they would first have to reflect upon what the students in their classroom already knew and where they needed to be going as readers and writers. But that wasn't a beginning either, because in order to reflect on their students, teachers would need to know (1) what kinds of things children generally know about language and (2) what strategies successful readers use.

We decided to begin there—Jan Toomes offered to write about what children know about language, and Donna Lindquist agreed to discuss reading as strategic. To provide a context for their understandings, they both decided to tell stories about readers they knew. By doing so, teachers could relate theory and research to real learners and understand how to make sense of the observations they were making in and out of their classrooms. Then Jan Toomes, Joan Gillette, and I would talk specifically about observing learners. It seemed important to share the kinds of questions we had developed to frame our observations. Becky Huntsman took on the challenge of explaining how response could build on these understandings and observations.

Once we had identified these pieces and begun to write, we became aware that just as there were ideas that led up to response, so too were there ideas that seem to follow from it. Response does not exist in isolation; it works as method only in an environment that facilitates communication. We decided to ask Noel Jones, a member of the faculty at the University of North Carolina at Wilmington, to talk about planning for literate environments and Jennifer Story, a local fifth- and sixth-grade language arts teacher who had received her master's degree the year before, to write about her decision making within the literate classroom environment she'd created.

In the process of writing this book, we've learned a lot. Sometimes our experiences allowed us to move past knowledge into understanding. We knew before we began, for example, that writing and reading were complementary processes. We'd read Smith (1985) and knew that it was important to "read like a writer" and "write like a reader"; for some of us, however, this was the first opportunity we'd really ever had to write. We learned that writing is a lot different when you care. As Jan wrote in her journal, "Writing when you really have something to say is HARD!"

Sometimes our experiences generated new insights. As writers, we had to find words for things we didn't know we knew, and for things we knew but had never shared. We saw that in the very process of thinking, of searching, we learned, we "outgrew our former selves" (Harste 1984). We began to understand that perhaps the best way to help others was to suggest they take some time to share what they know. We became advocates for reflective practice—for teachers to think about their beliefs and examine them critically, in light of what others believe.

That's how we hope you'll use this text—as a beginning point, the opening argument in a dialectic. What do you think about what we've said? Do you agree with what we think? Disagree? Why or why not? Do you think we've interpreted the literature correctly? Incorrectly? What would you do differently? Were the examples we've chosen effective? Useful? Was the text organized in a reasonable manner? How could it have been improved? Were there books and articles we should have cited but did not? Some we should have left out?

We hope you'll reflect on what we've written. We'd love to hear from you. Maybe the next edition could have contributions from teachers all over the country. Or perhaps you'd rather join forces with teachers you know and write your own volume.

We're convinced that teachers can make and are making a difference. We believe that education will improve as teachers begin to share with others what they know. Won't you help? We hope to hear your voice soon.

what matters?

IT MATTERS THAT TEACHERS UNDERSTAND HOW
LANGUAGE IS LEARNED

one

OBSERVING LEARNERS
What They Know About Language
Janine Toomes

Three-year-old Maggie carefully drew a large stick figure on the chalkboard. Underneath she wrote two long strings of random letters.

"Now," she said to me in an authoritative voice, "What does this say?" She waited patiently as I surveyed what she had written.

"Does it say *mom*?" I asked, basing my reply on what I took to be the figure's long curly hair.

"No!" she emphatically replied, running a pointer underneath the two lines of letters. "It says *grandmother* and *grandfather*."

Michael, also three years old, settled himself in a chair with one of his favorite books, *Mrs. Wishy-Washy* (Cowley & Melser 1980). Opening the book to the first page he briefly studied the picture and began to read aloud.

TEXT	MICHAEL
"Oh, lovely mud," said the cow, and she jumped in it.	*The cow jumped in the mud.*
"Oh, lovely mud," said the pig, and he rolled in it.	*The pig jumped in the mud and rolled over.*
"Oh, lovely mud," said the duck, and she paddled in it.	*The duck jumped in the mud.*
Along came Mrs. Wishy-Washy. "Just look at you!" she screamed.	*And Mrs. Wishy-Washy screamed at them. "Again! You jumped in the mud."*

Neither Maggie nor Michael have had contact with formal schooling, yet their actions and responses indicate that they already know a great deal about what it means to be literate. They are what Smith (1985, 124) calls "junior members of the literacy club." No one expects them, at age three, to be able to read and write like experienced members of the club; but no one doubts they will do so in time.

A keen observer of young children will realize that Maggie and Michael are not unique with respect to their knowledge about language and its use. They are the rule rather than the exception. Indeed, extensive research (Clark 1984; Clay 1975, 1979a/b; Doake 1985; Ferreiro & Teberosky 1982; Harste, Woodward & Burke 1984; Holdaway 1979; Voss 1988; Wells 1986) has documented the phenomenal growth children achieve naturally during the preschool years. Using Maggie and Michael as our informants, let us look back at their language stories and examine what they, and children like them, know about literacy.

What Children Know About Language

CHILDREN ARE ACCOMPLISHED ORAL-LANGUAGE USERS AND COMPREHENDERS

Children like Maggie and Michael were not *taught* to speak and use oral language. They *learned* over time, achieving their competence by being immersed in a community of oral-language users who encouraged them to participate as best as they could from the beginning, all the while supporting their experimentations and approximations (Cambourne 1984; Cambourne & Turbill 1987).

As children learn to talk, they not only learn the language, they also learn about language in general. They acquire a basic understanding of its rules, structures, and terminology (Goodman 1977). Finally, children learn through language. They use language as a tool to learn new information and to acquire the basic concepts necessary for understanding things, events, thoughts, and feelings. They talk to share, to seek help, to acquire the things they want, and to communicate their understandings. In particular, they talk about the literacy events in which they participate (Wells 1986). In this manner, oral and written language become interconnected, mutually reinforcing and supporting each other (Harste, Woodward, & Burke 1984).

Maggie and Michael provide clear examples. Both children used oral language to test and confirm their knowledge about written language. They did this naturally and freely, but in different ways. Maggie used oral language to request participation from me. She wanted to test her hypothesis that, yes, written language does carry meaningful messages that can be read and understood by others. Michael used oral language imaginatively as he created his personal version of *Mrs. Wishy-Washy*. His rendition of the story was evidence of the profound effects of repeated experience with literature. Oral language provided a medium for showing that he had internalized a sense of story, sound, and rhythm.

CHILDREN UNDERSTAND THE PURPOSES OF PRINT AND EXPECT IT TO BE MEANINGFUL

Maggie and Michael both showed signs of understanding that print serves a purpose and communicates meaning. Clay (1977) states that one way young children often test this process is by producing signs we cannot

4

Janine Toomes

interpret and then expecting us to read them. This is exactly what Maggie did when she requested that I read her "words." She waited patiently for me to read them because she fully expected me, someone who knew the "code," to be able to understand the meaning of her message.

Michael, too, expected that the print in *Mrs. Wishy-Washy* would be meaningful. It did not matter to him that his version of the story was not a word-for-word match with the actual text, as long as it made sense. It did, so he was perfectly content with his reading.

Goodman (1984) points out that such understanding develops as children participate in meaningful literacy events. They learn, through experience, that written language will make sense, whether it is writing on a chalkboard, in a book, or on a road sign. Such learning does not happen by chance. It is an intentional effort on the part of the child to experiment with a communication system they have seen work for those around them (Newman 1984). Once children have grasped the fact that all types of print are used to communicate meaning, they have learned the main concept required for reading and writing progress (Clay 1977).

CHILDREN ARE AWARE OF THE GRAPHIC SYSTEM
OF WRITTEN LANGUAGE

Maggie best illustrates this knowledge by her efforts to write the words *grandmother* and *grandfather.* She constructed her own spellings for the words based on what she understood about alphabetic form and the connections between speech and print. She wrote using correctly formed, though random, uppercase letters. Such atypical uses of letter case are not errors, but rather are illustrations of her awareness of the critical features in letter discrimination (Clark 1984). Maggie also chose to spell her words using two long lines of print. For her, the longer the word was orally, the more letters she needed to write.

Such gross approximations are characteristics of what Temple, Nathan, and Burris (1982) call prephonemic spelling. For Maggie and other children at this beginning level, letters do not yet represent sounds. As Maggie becomes more experienced with print, her writing will gradually change to a mixture of upper- and lowercase letters. She will also begin to show an increased awareness of the connections between letter and sound, as well as to show more sophisticated knowledge of linearity, directionality, spacing, sequencing patterns, forms, repetitions, and uniformity of size and shape (Clay 1975).

CHILDREN ARE COMFORTABLE WITH BOOKS, KNOW HOW THEY WORK, AND ARE AWARE OF BOOK LANGUAGE

Let us once again examine the reading-like behavior (Doake 1985; Holdaway 1979) of Michael. *Mrs. Wishy-Washy* was a book with which he had repeated experience, so he was quite comfortable with both the book and the story. He knew where to begin reading and turned the pages confidently and correctly. As he read he demonstrated control over the syntax of book language by using phrases and intonation patterns characteristic of books rather than of speech and by reading expressively and fluently, much like an accomplished adult reader. He also frequently referred to the pictures, depending on them to yield semantic clues as to how he should read the book. As a result, his version, while approximate, retained the gist of the story.

Chall (1983) refers to this sort of behavior as having a "schema emphasis"—that is, the child's attention is focused on using and getting meaning rather than matching the written words to the spoken sounds. Such behaviors often result when adults read, and reread, familiar stories to children, encouraging their active participation in the reading (Doake 1985). These literacy experiences are highly significant indicators of a child's developing knowledge about literacy.

CHILDREN ARE FLEXIBLE IN THEIR ATTEMPT TO USE AND LEARN ABOUT LANGUAGE

Young children quite naturally draw upon any available means of gaining a new perspective on the language they are attempting to use or comprehend. By combining any of the alternative functions of language (speaking, listening, reading, and writing) together with any of the other communication systems (such as drama, music, art, or math), they become more proficient in their attempt to clarify understandings. In this manner, literacy is "multimodal" (Harste, Woodward & Burke 1984).

For example, both Maggie and Michael depended on more than just print to construct meaning. Maggie drew her figure first, using it as a means of planning her writing. Her obviously female figure also provided the clue to determining the ultimate meaning of her "words." Michael also "played" at reading, relying on the pictures as guides for how he would read the book.

In an attempt to test further her hypotheses about written language,

Janine Toomes

Maggie sought to interact orally with someone who knew the written code. Such social interactions—that is, discussions with others prior to, during, or after a literacy event—are a natural part of the reading and writing process. They help children like Maggie to clarify, refine, and extend the meaning of a text.

The same factors are in force when children first begin reading environmental print. They use the situational context and their knowledge of the colors and shapes of signs and labels to know that the octagonal red sign says "Stop" or that the sign under the golden arches says "McDonald's." More often than not they verbally share these understandings quite proudly with whoever is near—just to make sure they are right. This ability to draw flexibly on alternative modes of expression and existing social systems is critical to all language users, no matter what age.

How Children Develop as Literate Individuals

Almost all children acquire language naturally, so much so that some children like Maggie and Michael begin reading and writing before they or their parents are even aware that they are becoming literate (Durkin 1966; Harste, Woodward, & Burke 1984; Goodman & Goodman 1979). The Maggies and Michaels of this world have acquired their knowledge about literacy because caring adults have interacted with them in a print-rich environment. These adults have read to them, talked with them, and provided many opportunities for them to experiment with oral and written language.

Admittedly, there will be those children who know less. For a variety of reasons, growth in language learning is not uniform among children, nor does it always progress in a linear fashion. Even under the best of conditions development is more likely to be sporadic and "messy." Sometimes progress is barely noticeable; other times it is quite dramatic. At still other times, a child constructing a new language rule may so concentrate on the new learning that he overgeneralizes and seemingly regresses elsewhere (Bissex 1980; Newman 1984).

To illustrate these inconsistencies, let us examine the written language development of eight-year-old Laura. When Laura first came to the Educational Laboratory at the University of North Carolina at Wilmington, her behavior suggested that she knew less about oral and written language than did either Michael or Maggie. Her mother commented that Laura was extremely reluctant to talk with people outside her immediate family

Dear Jan

I

Love

you

by

Laura

and that she had never shown any observable interest in print. As a result, Laura was identified as being "at risk" by the school system and was referred to our Ed Lab for tutoring services.

As staff of the Ed Lab, our goal was to understand and support Laura's efforts thoroughly as a learner and provide her with the same conditions necessary for language learning (Cambourne 1984; Cambourne & Turbill 1987) that Maggie and Michael experienced naturally.

For the first two months of instruction, Laura seemed crippled by her reluctance to take any risks. Every aspect of her behavior seemed constrained. She would not even cross the room without either her mother or her tutor by her side. When asked to write, her message was always the same—the words, the content, and even the few people to whom she would write (see Figure 1–1). Never once did she venture into the unknown.

A closer examination of her efforts revealed that Laura failed to understand many of the most basic concepts about print. The physical arrangement of the words was always vertical, rather than left to right and punctuation was nonexistent. More importantly, while a message was present in her notes, the content of the message remained identical for the entire two-month period, in spite of repeated requests from others to respond to the messages they sent her. Forward progress appeared to be nonexistent.

Janine Toomes

FIGURE 1-2

At the end of the second month, Laura made a sign requesting that the other students and tutors in the lab keep out of the room in which she was preparing to make a tape recording of a story she had practiced (see Figure 1–2).

On the surface, Laura's product appeared to be a dramatic regression from the previous messages. While words were spelled correctly, the placement of the words on the page was severely scrambled. She did not seem aware of the inconsistency even when asked to reread what she had written. At a deeper level, however, Laura's product represented a small step forward. For the first time she attempted to communicate a genuine message to the others in the lab. Perhaps it was her intense concentration on communicating the message that interfered with her ability to attend to surface-level inconsistencies.

During the third month at the lab, Laura began to bloom. A dramatic change appeared in the entries she made in a journal kept with her tutor (see Figure 1–3).

No longer was spelling correct. In fact, the entire entry relied heavily on invented spelling. To many, her product may have again appeared another step back. From our perspective, however, Laura's effort represented quite the opposite. At some point over the previous months Laura had internalized the concept that Maggie and Michael had already learned at age three—that it is the meaning being relayed rather than the correctness of the spelling that is of prime importance. Laura had truly taken a dramatic step forward!

During the fifth month of instruction, Laura wrote a new message, shown in Figure 1–4.

The figure shows a child's handwritten text with the conventional reading alongside:

tueddy I am
go to
my gram
So I
can hepe
on bese
she dute
fell gud
bees she
has a
cod and
I am
guw to
ask What
she wus
me to
do, and
my grap
was
sek now
he Is
bet
and he
com to
sed the nit with

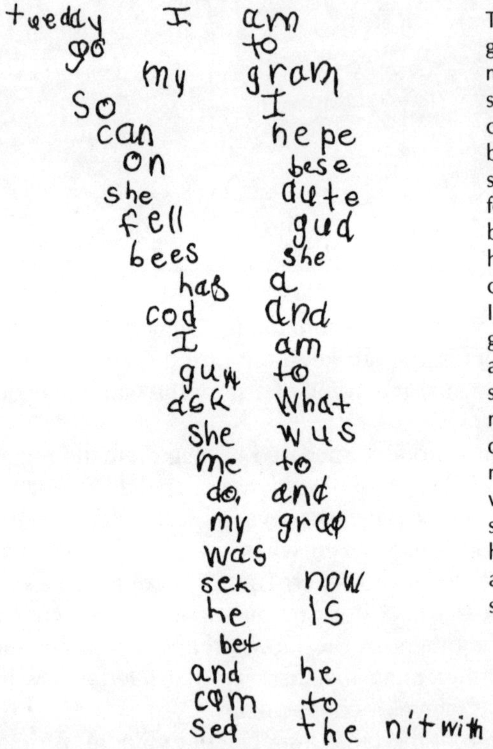

Tuesday I am
going to
my grandmother's
so I
can help
because
she doesn't
feel good
because she
has a
cold and
I am
going to
ask what
she wants
me to
do. And
my grandfather
was
sick. Now
he is better
and he came to
spend the night with us.

Janine Toomes

Laura's message is yet another indication of her progress. Spelling became conventional and her writing progressed from left to right. At the same time, she communicated a genuine message—a message appropriate for the situation and the receiver. What was unique about Laura's writing at this time was her sudden awareness of punctuation. She was so intent on using punctuation marks that she overgeneralized her language learning, putting marks everywhere. As with the invented spellings, such overgeneralizations will eventually disappear with proper support and continued experiences with print.

FIGURE 1-4

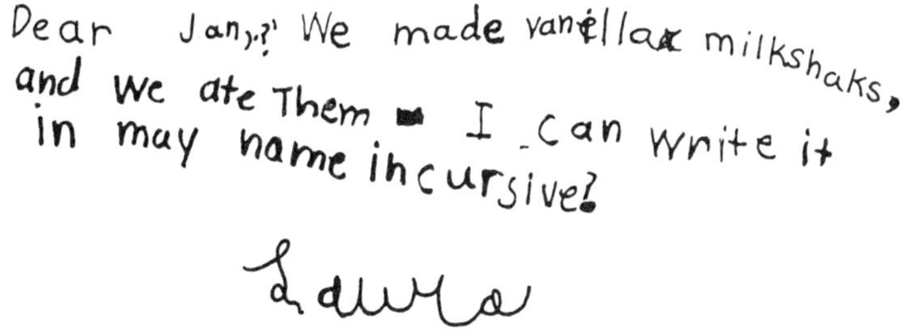

Dear Jany, We made vanella milkshaks,
and We ate Them ⚫ I can write it
in may name in cursive!

Laura

Laura's story illustrates two points. First, age is not an accurate determinant of a child's developmental level. Even when children enter school for the first time there will be a wide range of abilities and levels. Children arrive at school with an emergent literacy all their own (Minns 1988). Second, in the process of learning language, fluency is not some final state. When new learning is taking place, everyone, no matter what age, shows the same erratic pattern evident in Laura's writing. Thus, development is a continual process (Newman 1984). For these reasons, teachers need to be cautious about thinking of literacy development in terms of neat stages (Harste, Woodward & Burke 1984).

In a monumental nine-year longitudinal study in which he followed the language development and academic progress of thirty-two children from the age of fifteen months through their final year of elementary school, Gordon Wells (1986) found a strong relationship between a child's knowledge about literacy at age five and all later school achievements. In this respect, it becomes critical that teachers understand early language development and have a sense of what has transpired in order to be able to recognize a child's strengths. Teachers who possess such an understanding and believe that children like Maggie, Michael, and Laura are already functioning as readers and writers when they come to school, will be better able to develop a curriculum that recognizes and expands on each child's knowledge. A supportive curriculum is critical to facilitating the ongoing process of language learning.

Observing Learners

what matters?

IT MATTERS THAT TEACHERS UNDERSTAND THAT
READING IS STRATEGIC

INVITING THE LITERACY LEARNER TO ENGAGE IN READING

Donna B. Lindquist

Reading *Big Dog . . . Little Dog* (Eastman 1973), eight-year-old Jason scanned the picture that showed Fred and Ted painting a house. The text below read: "When they painted the house, Ted used red paint. Fred used green." When confronted with the unfamiliar word *house,* Jason skipped it, proceeded to finish the sentence, and then confidently went back to tackle the unfamiliar word.

"When they painted the horse, Ted used red paint." He paused and then muttered to himself, "No! That doesn't make sense." He glanced at the picture and then at the word, hesitated, smiled, and triumphantly announced, *"House,* that's it!" Happily he returned to the beginning of the text, successfully reread the two sentences with convincing fluency and intonation, and then proceeded to the next page, glancing at the picture and text before attempting to read it aloud.

What lessons can be gleaned from Jason's reading demonstration? First of all, Jason demonstrated his use of all of the major language cue systems—syntactic, semantic, and grapho-phonemic, as identified by Ken Goodman (1976). When faced with the unfamiliar word *house,* Jason's intuitive knowledge about grammar (syntax) helped him narrow the choices from which he could predict the unknown word. That he chose a noun and not an adverb indicates this syntactic awareness. He then looked at the word itself—that is, he used grapho-phonemic cues. The words *house* and *horse* would be identical except for the third letter. But because he had already used prediction to narrow down the number of possible alternatives, Jason, like a typical reader, then used only minimal visual (grapho-phonemic) information to identify tentatively the word. Jason's self-correction, *horse* to *house,* highlights his awareness that *horse* did not fit with the context of the story. Ken Goodman (1976) refers to these meaning cues as semantic information.

Just two weeks before reading *Big Dog . . . Little Dog,* Jason had been referred to the Ed Lab, the university's after-school program, because he had a CAT (California Achievement Test) score in the first percentile. The school wondered if he was retarded. As I observed Jason's struggles with the printed words, I realized from his demonstrated reading performance that he was not making strategic use of all of the cue systems in language—syntactic, grapho-phonemic and semantic. To help him develop this understanding, I began by providing Jason with numerous literacy demonstrations in which I modeled successful reading strategies (prediction, sampling, confirmation/correction, skipping over unknown words in order to make sense from the context) in a variety of situations and contexts.

Inviting the Literacy Learner to Engage in Reading

The following dialogue took place on the second day of our sessions, and it illustrates how this "cue check" process is facilitated. The book is *Where's Spot* (Hill 1980), and on one page Spot is shown peering at a large piece of furniture with glass doors.

Jason: (*Reading*) "IS HE IN THE WINDOW?"
Donna: Yes, it does look like a window. But open it up. What's inside?
Jason: (*Opens doors*) The monkey.
Donna: Yes, the monkey is inside. What is he doing?
Jason: He's eating a banana and hanging from something.
Donna: Good. What else is hanging from the rod?
Jason: A clothes hanger.
Donna: Yes, and where do you find clothes hangers?
Jason: In a closet.
Donna: That's right. Let's look again at the word (*closet*). Do you still think that *window* makes sense here?
Jason: No. It's *closet*. (*Reading*) "IS HE IN THE CLOSET?"
Donna: Great. I like the way you used your brain to figure it out by yourself.
Jason: (*Both pleased and awed with himself*) I did.

As I helped Jason become aware of which strategies he was using, he learned to self-monitor his reading behavior and eventually replaced the less successful strategies with more proficient ones. Once this happened, Jason realized he was a reader and that he, indeed, had the words in his head (Lindquist 1988).

As teachers work one-on-one with "readers at risk," they soon become proficient in observing which strategies learners use to make sense of print and in helping them learn to self-monitor those strategies.

The most important question a teacher can ask a reader or writer is, "Does that make sense?" Learners need to be encouraged to ask the same question of themselves as they read and write. (K. Goodman 1986, 40)

They also discover that these strategies help readers of all ages construct meaning from print. Adult beginning reader Jerry read, "Sometimes they carry houses to the show grounds," despite the accompanying photo clearly showing *horses* by the *horse* trailers at a fairground.

Donna: Wait a minute. Did you hear what you just read?
Jerry: (*Confused and without looking up at the picture*) "Sometimes they carry houses to the showgrounds."

Donna: Let's check the picture. [confirmation strategy]

Jerry: (*Embarrassed*) Oh! Excuse me. "Sometimes they carry *horses* to the show grounds!" [correction strategy]

Donna: Yes!

Jerry: That makes more sense.

Donna: The words are almost alike, aren't they? Let's look. (*I write them.*)

Jerry: (*Points to third letter of each*) That's the only difference.

Donna: I'm glad you figured that out. What a difference it makes!

It is particularly striking that the same words—*horse(s)* and *house(s)*—were confused by both eight-year-old Jason and fifty-six-year-old Jerry. It also seems that while both were concentrating on syntactic and grapho-phonemic cues, in these particular instances, Jason made more effective use of self-monitoring strategies than did Jerry. Jason realized a sentence later that what he had read didn't sound right and went back to confirm and correct. In contrast, Jerry didn't even "hear" what he had read; he automatically went on to the next page.

Nine-year-old Suzy, labeled by the school as "dyslexic," cringed when asked to read. In the initial interview, Suzy's mother expressed concern about Suzy's role in the family. As the youngest of three, she was often able to plead helpless and thus encourage her older siblings to come to her rescue. Consequently, she lacked confidence in making her own decisions.

I spent part of our first tutoring session getting acquainted with Suzy, trying to understand her as a learner. As we talked, I steered the conversation toward how it felt to be the youngest child in the family. She was enthusiastic as we talked about the different perspectives of the oldest and youngest, including the stereotypic descriptions of the oldest "knowing everything and being the greatest," while the youngest was often thought of as "a pain."

The cover of *The Pain and the Great One* (Blume 1974) depicts the profiles of a scheming younger boy plotting back-to-back with his smug older sister. Blume's book deals with a "great" oldest sister and a young "pain" of a brother—a situation similar to Suzy's experience in her own family. By discussing Suzy's situation, I hoped to help her pick up on the semantic or meaning cues in the text.

As Suzy began to read the title, her countenance wilted into a frown. As I watched, I sensed our previous conversation evaporate away. This feeling was confirmed as she haltingly read *"The* Plan *and the Great One."* I responded to what she had read. "Look at the picture of the sister and brother. You read *'The* Plan *and the Great One.'* Does that make sense?" She shrugged her shoulders.

As she began reading the text—hesitantly, barely audibly and with increasing anxiety—it was apparent to me that she was intensely suffering the word she had missed: *pain.* It was also evident that she did not feel good about herself as a reader and had added her own label of "failure" next to the one assigned by the specialists years ago.

I tried demonstrating how to predict the text using both pictures and context clues. Suzy was definitely interested in the pictures. "What's that?" she repeatedly asked as she flipped through the pages. I told her that we'd read and find out. "Where do you think we'll find the answers to your questions about the story?" I queried. She responded, "In the back of the book."

To a "kidwatcher" (Y. Goodman 1978), armed with an understanding of the cue systems described earlier, Suzy's shrug and her other responses in our first reading session strongly suggested that she was not looking for meaning, but, instead, was relying too heavily upon syntactic and grapho-phonemic cues. Suzy's prior experiences with reading had convinced her that "getting it right" was more important than making sense.

A reader's task is to make meaning from the printed page. What Suzy didn't understand was that meaning doesn't radiate from the printed word as one gazes at the text. There is no automatic and instantaneous mental process of understanding the author's intentions. That's why prior knowledge (schemata) is so important; reading is a transaction between writer and reader.

In our second session, Suzy began to discover this for herself. Suzy's mother was an airline flight attendant; Suzy had flown extensively and was quite familiar with airports and airplane terminology. Yet, when confronted with the text accompanying a picture book narrating a young boy's plane flight, she did not seem to make connections between the words she was reading and the concepts she knew. Instead, she focused on individual words, trying to break them into syllables by using her fingers to block out segments of the word. As I encouraged her to use her prior knowledge to make predictions, she began to shift her focus from examining a word in isolation to putting it within the context of the story, using the pictures to support her predictions. She seemed both pleased and confident as she easily read passages containing words such as *terminal, security, flyer, dial,* and *instrument.* Suzy understood the concepts these words represented and now had a new reading strategy.

Suzy's mother seemed to define good readers as people who get all the words "right." As she had explained in the initial interview, "Suzy is an excellent reader, but she doesn't know what she's reading." However, as Suzy was discovering for herself, reading is a lot more than knowing words. It is a process of constructing meaning from the text—a process that is affected by many factors.

One important factor is the reader's view of reading. Suzy's remark "in the back of the book" suggested that she viewed reading as a passive, rather than active, process. A learner who has actively engaged in real literacy events, using language to communicate with others, unconsciously develops an understanding of the reading process. When literacy events are real and meaningful, children, like Michael and Maggie, are interested in engaging as readers and writers and so begin to learn about written language. Suzy's response that she would look for answers in the back of the book suggested that her prior reading experiences were focused more upon being "right" than being real.

The information that the reader brings to the text is a second important factor. The reader brings a wealth of experience and knowledge *to* print. The process of making meaning *from* print cannot proceed fluently if the reader lacks background knowledge. Suzy's wealth of knowledge and experiences enabled her to make a meaningful connection with the print in the airline book. In contrast, Jason could not identify the word *closet* even with the picture cue because he had probably never seen an antique clothes closet. Simply stated, one cannot take from the printed page what one has not brought to it.

A third influence on reading is the reader's willingness to take risks. Risk taking is critical to the reading/learning process. Consider Jerry's experience: he and I had been reading books on trucks and the intricate process involved in paving a road. In our reading, we had learned that metal was sometimes used in the paving process. One day, Jerry mentioned that he was responsible for getting the parking lot paved at his church and that he had asked the paving contractor if metal would be used. The contractor explained how metal was used in different areas of the country but not in our coastal area. Jerry went on to tell the contractor that he had read about metal in a book about paving. Jerry seemed pleased that he had been able to use what he read and that he was able to demonstrate to the contractor that he was a reader.

Inviting the Literacy Learner to Engage in Reading

Jerry had long believed that he couldn't write. However, I took advantage of his obviously improved self-esteem, grabbed a sheet of paper, and engaged him in our first "written conversation" (Burke 1985). Although my sentences were initially simple and involved a "yes" or "no" reply, within minutes I was providing him with conventionally spelled words that he used to expand the length and sophistication of his responses.

Moments later he confidently chose to tackle an unfamiliar book. As he read the word *wall,* he looked up at me with an astounded expression. *"Wall?"* he began. "Is that right? That's the first time I've seen that word. And I read it!"

After two months of twice-weekly, hour-long instruction, Jerry had begun to take risks. His expression of obvious joy and accomplishment replaced his all-too-frequent looks of dread, fear, and indecision. Jason's reading progress also soared after he began to take risks and Suzy's self-esteem improved dramatically and she exhibited less anxiety once she felt free to risk reading.

Reading instruction is a fourth critical influence on reading. Learners infer their definitions of reading from what is emphasized during reading instruction (Harste, Woodward & Burke 1984). Because Suzy thought that the answers were "in the back of the book," it was critical that she be provided with an environment that would allow her to discover that this wasn't so. Teachers who understand that reading is a strategic process establish environments that provide opportunities for children to learn language and learn about language while they are using language for real purposes (Halliday 1973). In such classrooms, reading is a social event in which prediction, sampling, and confirmation are considered essential to the learning process. Risk taking is encouraged and teachers frequently communicate to the students that they believe in them as learners. In so doing, they help the students to believe in themselves.

Effective teachers know about language, literacy, and instruction. Effective teachers also know a great deal about the children with whom they work. Informed observation is therefore central to the teachers' decision-making process.

20

Donna B. Lindquist

what matters?

IT MATTERS THAT TEACHERS MAKE
INFORMED OBSERVATIONS

three

BUILDING ON WHAT MATTERS

Janine Toomes, Diane Stephens, and Joan Gillette

Once teachers understand how language learning occurs, have a sense of what matters about the reading process itself, and are confident that children can function as readers and writers, the next task is to understand the learners. This is best done through keen, careful, and informed observation.

To be an effective "kidwatcher" (Y. Goodman 1985), teachers must go far beyond monitoring only correct and incorrect responses (Bussis 1982). For example, fifth-grader Jed came to the Educational Lab at the University of North Carolina at Wilmington with a history of difficulties with spelling. According to school records, he was able to complete successfully the exercises accompanying each word list in the spelling book, but he consistently failed each and every spelling test on Friday. In addition, his spelling on written work was "atrocious." This type of information, focused on the end product of instruction, provided little insight into Jed's difficulties. It told us only what Jed was not doing; to help him, we needed to know what he could do and how he accomplished that.

Along with many others (Bussis 1982; Clay 1979; Y. Goodman 1978, 1985; Harste, Woodward & Burke 1984; Johnson 1987; Rhodes and Dudley-Marling 1988; Stephens 1989), we believe that helping learners begins with watching, listening to, and reflecting upon the strategies learners use during their attempts to apply knowledge and skill to realistic situations. In other words, as observers, we should focus on the process of learning rather than on the product. Such observation is much more likely to yield clues to learners' understandings and/or misconceptions, as well as to the ways they approach literacy tasks. If Jed's school records had provided information as to the strategies he used when spelling and the conditions under which he *could* spell words correctly, we would have had a much better understanding of how to help Jed overcome his difficulties.

Observing the nature of learners' understandings and strategies takes on even greater importance when we realize that although young children may not be able to explain what they know, they often demonstrate their knowledge in literacy-based tasks. In chapter one, for example, we have seen how Maggie and Michael's actions revealed their understandings about language—understandings that they, at their young ages, most certainly could not have verbalized.

Observation is an invaluable source of information. It enables teachers to tap into children's current knowledge and concepts by interpreting what they do and how they do it (McKenzie 1986). However, the real

Building on What Matters

essence of kid watching is a recursive pattern of hypothesizing, planning, observing, reflecting, and taking action. Stephens (1989) refers to this pattern as a hypothesis-test approach to curriculum.

The cycle begins when the teacher forms hypotheses about individual learners based on (1) what matters about language, learning, children, and the reading process (i.e. current theory); and (2) what the teacher needs to know about the learner in relation to that theory. Once these hypotheses are formed, the teacher creates an instructional plan that engages the learner as a reader and writer and allows for observation. During observation the teacher not only watches and listens, but also documents the learner's behaviors. Following observation, the teacher compares what has been observed with the original hypotheses—an analysis that in turn informs instruction and environmental design, and gives the teacher clues as to the best manner in which to provide support for the learner. At this point, one cycle is complete. However, due to the ever-changing nature of the learner, the cycle must continually repeat itself. Therefore, new hypotheses are formed or previous hypotheses that have not yet been fully answered are continued, and the cycle begins once more (see Figure 3–1).

Through informed observation, teachers can develop an understanding of their students as learners, have a guide for making instruction decisions, and increase the likelihood that their responses to students will be helpful.

Where, then, do teachers begin as they seek to become effective observers of learners? Teachers begin by seeking answers to many questions. Whether these questions are global or specific, they all attempt to get at the heart of what learners understand, feel, and do when confronted with a literacy task.

In the course of writing this book we spent many hours discussing the factors that we believe contribute to learners' growth in reading. Influenced by our reading (Clay 1975, 1979a, 1979b; Harste, Woodward, and Burke 1984; Holdaway 1979; Jagger and Smith-Burke 1985; Rhodes and Dudley-Marling 1988; Smith 1985; Weaver 1988) and by our observations of at-risk students (both children and adults), we concluded that to ensure literacy growth, learners needed to

1. Understand reading.
2. Believe in themselves as readers.
3. Build on what they know.
4. Be strategic.
5. Be willing to take risks.

24

Janine Toomes,
Diane Stephens, and
Joan Gillette

FIGURE 3-1

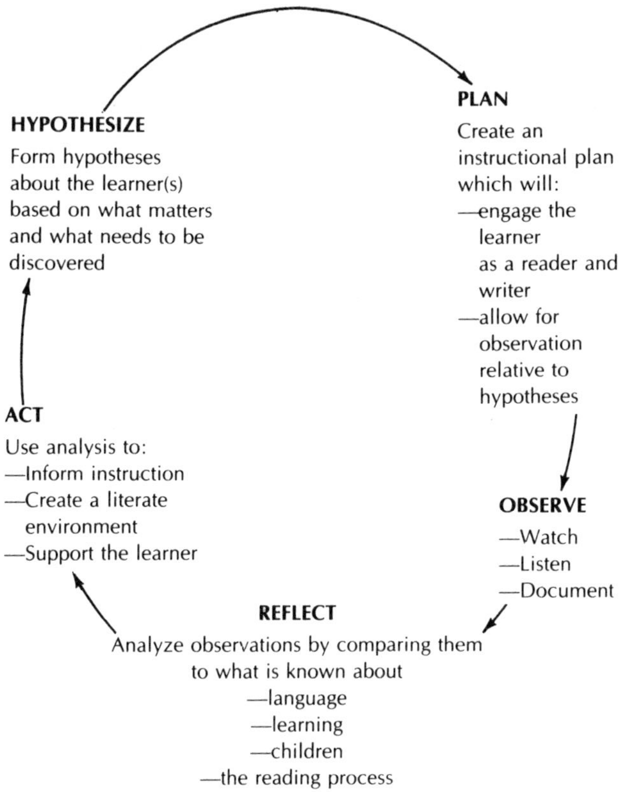

HYPOTHESIZE
Form hypotheses
about the learner(s)
based on what matters
and what needs to be
discovered

PLAN
Create an
instructional plan
which will:
—engage the
learner
as a reader and
writer
—allow for
observation
relative to
hypotheses

ACT
Use analysis to:
—Inform instruction
—Create a literate
environment
—Support the learner

OBSERVE
—Watch
—Listen
—Document

REFLECT
Analyze observations by comparing them
to what is known about
—language
—learning
—children
—the reading process

Understanding Reading

The first day eight-year-old Daryl came to the lab for tutoring he came armed with the "primer" he used in school. He was expecting Joan, his tutor, to teach him to read that book. According to his mother, he'd read the other books at this level and this was the only text the teacher had left to use. "The teacher doesn't know what to do with him," she explained, "because he hasn't been able to read this reader very well." Despite Daryl's being armed and ready, he didn't seem very enthusiastic about the reader. Although he asked to read "the next story" aloud, his attention seemed to wander and he frequently lost his place on the page. Often, he substituted words that didn't make sense.

Joan wondered how Daryl viewed reading. She asked him questions about things he read at home and found out that he thought reading was just something you did in a reading group. He didn't read outside of school and didn't seem to have had much experience being read to. He didn't know why people would choose to read and he clearly didn't see himself as a reader. By talking with Daryl, Joan also found out that he wasn't interested in the stories he'd been assigned. He did not want to read about "dogs that ran" and "cats that jumped." Instead, he liked dinosaurs, Cub Scouts, insects, and jokes.

Joan decided to help Daryl understand reading. Together they talked about what Daryl already knew about dinosaurs. He was, it turned out, quite an expert. Then they selected several dinosaur books. At first Joan read to Daryl. After reading and sharing several books, Joan then chose a book with a predictable pattern and illustrations that corresponded with the text. This time she and Daryl shared the reading. When he left that afternoon, he asked to take the book to his teacher, to share with her what he'd learned about dinosaurs—and to show her how he could read!

Daryl's story is not unique. Many of the individuals we saw in the lab initially considered reading as a rather unpleasant chore. They had limited experiences with books outside of school and had not had the opportunity to explore the world of books or to discover that reading is a way of knowing more about oneself and the world. They did not know that reading taps the mind and opens up new possibilities. Sometimes this meant they said they did not like to read when, in reality, they did not yet know what reading was all about.

To determine what learners do understand about reading, teachers can ask themselves the following:

1. Do the learners view reading as a real, purposeful activity rather than as something done only in school?
2. Do the learners understand reading to be a meaning-making process as opposed to the ability to "say the words right"?
3. To what extent do the learners view reading as an enjoyable experience? Do they talk about books they read or listen to? Do they look at books on their own?
4. Do the learners understand that we read for a variety of purposes? To learn? For enjoyment? To manage our world?

Janine Toomes,
Diane Stephens, and
Joan Gillette

5. What do the learners know about how books work? Do they know where to start? That there is a front and back to the book? Title? Author? Illustrator?

   Do the learners understand there is a relationship between what is written and what is said? That the story comes from what is on the page and from what they know?

   Do the learners understand the directional rules of printed language? That the text is read from left to right? Top to bottom?

   Do the learners understand the print components? Word? Letter? Sentence? Upper- and lowercase letters? Function of space? Uses of punctuation?
6. Do the learners understand that consistency exists in the text? For example, that *dinosaur* always says "dinosaur"?

   Is the learner aware of the difference that may exist in text structure? For example, that a social studies text is structurally different from a novel or poem and that each make unique demands upon the reader?

Believing in Self as Reader

Any teacher who engages in careful observation will quickly come to realize that it is critical for learners to possess a positive belief in themselves as readers. Indeed, such a notion is found in current reading research (Johnson 1987; Stephens 1987). Routman (1988) relates the story of how the "slow" readers in her remedial class wanted to read a book far above their measured reading level. To her surprise, she discovered that by letting them read this book and similar good literature and by offering her support and guidance, these students developed confidence in themselves as readers, which contributed greatly to their overall progress.

By contrast, lack of a positive self-concept can be a serious impediment to real reading progress. Learners who do not see themselves as members of the literacy club often unconsciously place constraints upon themselves (Smith 1985). Indeed, many of the children and adults who are referred to clinics or labs for diagnosis and remediation feel that there is something "wrong" with themselves, that they may never read or write like other people. We found this to be true for fourteen of the sixteen first graders who attended the UNC-Wilmington Ed Lab during the summer of 1987. This was also true for the adults we encountered who were having difficulty with literacy tasks.

*Building on What
Matters*

Cliff, one adult who attended the Ed Lab, had tried repeatedly over the years to find help. He wanted desperately to learn to read so that he could start his own business. He was a bright man and yet had been previously told that he would never learn to read. Frequently labeled "dyslexic" and/or "unteachable," Cliff thought that he would never be "right." So wounded was his ego that he felt this attempt at learning was his last chance. Afraid of being wrong, of reading "wrong," he was reluctant to use context or syntax as clues to meaning and, when it was suggested that he use his background and knowledge of the world to make sense of print, he became anxious. When asked to keep a daily record of his reading, he refused. He risked little in reading and risked nothing in writing. Like many others, Cliff's difficulties with learning to read and his poor self-concept were intimately connected.

To begin to probe learners' beliefs about themselves as readers, the teacher observes to discover answers to the following questions:

1. Do the learners seem to believe that they can succeed at reading? Do they show obvious signs of enjoying reading? Or do they seem to be defeated or helpless, showing signs of heightened emotional reaction when attempting to read?
2. Under what circumstances do the learners view themselves as effective readers? Never? When supported during shared reading? While reading independently? When reading texts (newspapers, magazines, manuals, books) related to an interest area?
3. How accurate are the learners' assessments of their abilities? Do they choose books of appropriate difficulty? Do they set reasonable goals for themselves?
4. What motivates the learners? True interest and enjoyment? Or the desire to impress significant others or to receive external rewards?
5. Are the learners actively engaged in their own learning or do they function as passive recipients, placing the responsibility for learning on someone else? Do they feel responsible for their learning difficulties or blame someone else?

Janine Toomes,
Diane Stephens, and
Joan Gillette

Building on What the Learner Knows

One advantage of being a close observer of children and adult learners is that the teacher is better able to capitalize on individual strengths, particularly with respect to interests and knowledge about topics being studied. Many times as we interacted with our at-risk students we found that capitalizing on these factors was really the *only* way to begin unlocking the defense mechanisms our learners had devised for themselves.

When fourteen-year-old Max first came to the lab he wasn't interested in either reading or writing. He focused instead on dropping out of school when he was sixteen. While getting to know Max, Stacy, his tutor, discovered that he loved fishing and wanted to build his own fishing pier when he left school. To help Max realize that reading and writing could be personally useful to him, Stacy capitalized on his long-range goal by helping him begin a "Pier Project."

They began by talking about what Max already knew about fishing piers from his experience of fishing on them with his father. Next they listed the information Max wanted to know about building piers and researched it in the university library. Max also wrote to, and actually visited, the owner of a local fishing pier. Then, by using the information he had collected, Max designed and wrote about his future pier. For the first time, he saw a reason to read and write. He also saw a reason for school. Having discovered that building a pier would take a lot of money, he decided to go to college so he could get a good job; then he would be able to make the money needed to build the pier!

A second and equally important result of close observation is that the teacher is better able to help readers use what they already know in order to understand the text or to decode unknown words. Often learners possess the tools they need to overcome difficulties, but are unable to use them.

For example, while reading a child's book, *Cars and How They Go* (Cole 1983), Alan, a forty-one-year-old mechanic who'd been labeled dyslexic, encountered a passage in the text that explained that cars "make power by burning gasoline. The gas vapor goes from the carburetor to the cylinders." Alan hesitated over the word *cylinder* and tried unsuccessfully to sound it out. Diane, his tutor, asked him not to look at the word but instead tell her what happens to the gas in a gasoline engine. He explained that the gas went from the carburetor to the intake, the head, or the cylinder. She then asked him to look back at the text to see whether the author had written *intake, head,* or *cylinder.* He glanced at the text and replied, "Oh, it says *cylinder.*"

Diane went on to explain that a lot of reading is simply using what you already know. Alan replied that he often got stuck trying to sound out words "like a record needle sticks" but that other tutors had told him that he shouldn't think about what the word could be. "That's guessing," Alan noted, "and you're not supposed to guess at reading."

To understand and assist learners in building on what they know, the observant teacher must seek to determine the following:

1. What kinds of world knowledge do the learners bring to the learning situation?
2. To what extent do the learners make connections between world knowledge and the text? Do the learners demonstrate an understanding of these connections by making comments that relates the text to their own lives? By raising relevant questions about the text? By sharing related information with others? By engaging in independent thinking?

Being Strategic

Good readers use a variety of strategies for dealing with the text. As they read, they monitor their progress and understanding, and make predictions about what is to follow. Then they either confirm those predictions or make corrections when their expectations are not verified or when miscues interfere with the meaning being constructed (K. Goodman 1976; Newman 1985).

Larry is a fourth grader who commented in the initial interview that he had a reading problem because he "couldn't sound out words." While reading *Dirt Bike Racer* (Christopher 1979), Larry read the word *commercials* as "cam-circles" and *scuba man* as "scub man." Neither miscue fit the meaning of the text. Upon closer examination of these miscues and others, we hypothesized that although Larry did make use of some grapho-phonemic knowledge, namely initial and final consonants, he inconsistently applied this knowledge and seemed generally unaware that other strategies could be employed to assist in decoding unknown words. As a result, he regularly substituted anything for an unrecognizable word based solely on this one strategy, "grabbing" at the word, rather than stopping to analyze it based on a flexible use of a variety of cue systems. We recorded no examples of self-correction and that, coupled with the fact that Larry appeared undisconcerted when the text did not make sense, caused us to hypothesize that Larry was not a strategic reader.

In order to help learners become strategic readers, the teacher first must determine the following:

30

*Janine Toomes,
Diane Stephens, and
Joan Gillette*

1. What strategies do the learners use *before* reading? Are they able to assess a learning task and accurately understand what may make it easy or hard? Do they devise a logical plan for attacking the task? Do they follow through with that plan?
2. What strategies do the learners use *during* reading? Do they make predictions based on picture clues, syntax, semantics, morphological clues, grapho-phonemic knowledge, understanding of story grammar?

    Do they self-monitor? Are they aware of when they do not understand what is being read? What action do they take? (For example, when they encounter an unrecognizable word, do they attempt to "sound it out"? Substitute a word with similar meaning? Skip it? Skip it and return to it later?)

    Do they vary reading rate according to the type of material? Do they use strategies such as skimming or scanning at appropriate times?
3. What strategies do the learners use *after* reading? Do they share the information and their reactions with others? Store the information for later use? Reject it as unimportant? Independently seek other materials related to the topic?
4. To what degree do the learners make use of social interactions with others or of alternate expressions (art, music, drama, or writing) in an attempt to clarify and extend their understanding of the text at any point during the process? Which helps them the most?
5. As a whole, which of the above strategies are the learners aware of that they can use? Which do they actually use? How flexibly?

Willingness to Take Risks

One reason individuals might be reluctant to engage in school learning tasks, apart from boredom, is risk. In order to learn you must take a chance (Smith 1985). For those learners who are willing to take the risk to test their own personal hypotheses about how to use and apply strategies to literacy-based tasks, growth will occur, especially when their efforts are supported by an informed, observant teacher. However, for those learners who find themselves reluctant to take a chance due to anxiety or repeated failure, development can be blocked.

Consider Carol and John. Carol looks up from a word she cannot read and begins talking about something completely unrelated to the text. When asked to attempt the word, she ignores the request and continues her chatter. John sits at his desk, unresponsive to the task in front of him. When the teacher approaches and urges him to begin, he says, "Why should I try? It won't do any good. I'll get it wrong anyway."

For these individuals, as well as for Laura in chapter one, Suzy in chapter two, and Alan and Cliff in this chapter, literacy-based tasks are often a real struggle. They believe that no matter how hard they might try, failure is inevitable. In the severe cases, these learners may stop trying altogether in an effort to avoid additional failure—even when given a chance to succeed. As teachers, we must help these learners overcome their fears and take the risks so necessary to literacy growth.

To understand a learner's willingness to take risks, the teacher must determine the following:

1. Under what conditions do the individuals choose to read?
2. To what degree are they willing to take risks to independently guess at unknown words? Select a book? Make predictions? Talk about what they have read? Choose to pursue a topic of interest?
3. Do the learners ever become handicapped by the fear of making mistakes resulting in a refusal to try? Developing avoidance behaviors? Depending on significant others for needed information?
4. To what degree does the willingness to take risks vary with the situation? Social setting (group as opposed to individual)? Subject matter?

Making it Work

32

*Janine Toomes,
Diane Stephens, and
Joan Gillette*

While these questions are by no means exhaustive, they can serve as a starting point for discovering more about learners and the reading process. Because learners are unique, the real questions to be asked will vary according to the individual and the situation.

Teachers who want to become effective "kidwatchers" (Y. Goodman 1985) must realize that taking an observational approach to understanding learners entails far more than sitting back and waiting for all of their questions to be answered. The recursive cycle of observation is a skill that requires both expertise and practice (Rhodes and Dudley-Marling 1988), as well as teachers who are willing to become advocates and active listeners (Johnson 1987).

To make observation work, teachers need to keep several guidelines in mind:

1. Observation must be ongoing (Watson 1985). It must be done consistently and over a period of time, as well as in different situations (Rhodes and Dudley-Marling 1988).
2. The setting, as well as learners' reading and writing behaviors, needs to be considered. This includes the physical setting, the person initiating the activity, the instructions given, and the teacher's own behavior (Rhodes and Dudley-Marling 1988).
3. Records of observations need to be kept for future study. These may be done in the form of notes kept cooperatively with the learner (Atwell 1987), hypothesis-test sheets (Stephens in press), or check-sheets (Bailey et al. 1988; Harp 1988).
4. Observations of learners need not be unobtrusive (Rhodes and Dudley-Marling 1988). When the learner is successful at some task, it may be desirable for the teacher to move in and extend the activity (Y. Goodman 1985).
5. During the time the learners are involved in a task, it may be useful for the teacher to ask questions to verify what is being observed (Rhodes and Dudley-Marling 1988), to help the learners reflect on their own thinking, or to provide assistance when they become frustrated (Y. Goodman 1985).

Used optimally, observation is a critical factor in the educational process, and the teacher is the real key to making it work. Teachers who continually observe and reflect on what they discover about the learners' understandings about reading, beliefs about self, ability to build on what is known, strategicness, and willingness to take risks will find themselves much more knowledgeable about the individuals they teach. They will also be able to make better judgments about environmental arrangements, lesson design, and even the very manner in which they will respond to the learners. What greater benefits can there be than these!

*Building on What
Matters*

what matters?

IT MATTERS THAT TEACHERS USE RESPONSE TO
SUPPORT LEARNING

four

QUESTIONING AND RESPONDING

Rebecca Huntsman

Effective teachers use questions and responses to teach. Weaving their understandings about learners, language, and reading into instruction, they seize the teachable moment and respond spontaneously to learners. Questions and responses are not predetermined, not written down to be read at the "appropriate" time. Effective teachers capitalize on the teachable moment, using the opportunity when interest is highest to introduce an idea, elaborate on a question, or highlight one aspect of language. Throughout this chapter, specific examples of effective responses will be cited in order to illustrate this teaching technique. For instance, in response to one five-year-old child who thought quotation marks signaled a question, Mrs. O'Brian, one of the teachers on the Wright Group story box tape (1987) commented:

It's a little bit like a question mark, but it isn't a question mark. . . . But you were looking and you were thinking. These two marks here are showing us that the pig is talking to us. They're called speech marks.

When inviting students to work on follow-up assignments, she participated in the following exchange:

Mrs. O'Brian: Triangles can go to painting. Treat, you're the triangle leader.
Treat: T for Treat.
Mrs. O'Brian: T for Treat and *t* for triangle, that's right!

Responding to an adult who had previously used just one word, *electric,* for *electric, electrical,* and *electricity* but then discovered the word *electrical* in his reading, another teacher explained:

Electrical *is used to describe the motor. It's called an adjective. Adjectives are word forms that describe.* Electrical *is an adjective and so is the word* electric. *Then there's another form,* electricity, *that's a noun.* Electricity *is what travels through the wire;* electrical *is the kind of motor you are reading about. (Stephens, D. April 1988. Personal Communication).*

These teachers, teachers of both children and adults, are effective because they recognize the teachable moment, and through their responses, they build on it when it occurs.

Questioning and Responding

Questions

Just as prediction is essential to effective reading, putting to use what readers already know is essential to prediction. Readers must relate the present to the past in order to anticipate the future. Effective questions can help students tap into their knowledge and feelings associated with out-of-school experiences. Consider the following examples:

What do bee hives have inside them? (Honey). Yes, and what else do they have inside them? (Bees). Bees, right! How would you feel if you were a bee and your bee hive were hit with a bommy knocker? (Wright Group 1987)

How would you feel, what would you do, if you were trapped inside a cave full of rattlesnakes? (Huntsman, Feb. 1988. Personal Communication)

You know a lot about engines. What would happen after the spark plug fired? (Stephens, D. 1988. Personal Communication)

QUESTIONS TO CREATE ENJOYMENT, ENCOURAGE THINKING, AND
HELP LEARNERS MAKE THEIR OWN DISCOVERIES

Most educators agree that discovering something on our own is more powerful than simply being supplied with the same information. Readers who are excited and engaged as learners are more apt to make their own discoveries. Effective questions can provide the impetus for excitement, for thinking, and for discovery.

Teacher: Do you think this story could really happen, Alex?
Child: Hmmmm. It might and it might not.
Teacher: Why do you think it might happen?
Child: Because that caterpillar ate a hole in something every day, so I think it might be able to happen because he only ate one hole in it.
Teacher: Um hmmm.
Child: He didn't eat the whole thing; he only ate one hole. And he ate it day by day; he didn't eat all of it in one day. So I think it could happen.

38

Rebecca Huntsman

Teacher: Why did you think maybe it couldn't happen?

Child: On the other chance, 'cause caterpillars might not be that hungry.

Teacher: You mean this caterpillar was real hungry?

Child: Andrea, I have a way we could find out.

Teacher: How? How could we find out?

Child: You could leave a lot of fruit and stuff out like this. [pause]

Teacher: Um hmmm.

Child: And leave it out there all night.

Teacher: Um hmmm.

Child: And come back in the morning and see if there are a couple of little holes in it.

Teacher: Yeah. And then we could find out. Do you think maybe if there were holes in it, it might be a caterpillar eating it?

Child: Well, we could find out by slicing it open.

Teacher: Aha. See if he was inside eating? That's a good idea, Alex.
(Genishi, McCarrier & Nussbaum, 1988)

QUESTIONS TO MAKE CHILDREN AWARE OF WRITING AS A CRAFT

Readers need to know that authors write for many reasons and that writers have problems and make choices as they write. Effective teachers help students view writing as a craft by helping them become aware of the various techniques that authors use in order to communicate effectively with readers. Effective questions can acquaint students with authors' problems and choices, as well as with larger themes and social issues.

What does this kind of print tell us? (Wright Group 1987)

Can you begin to figure out what the animals and piranha might represent to him? Can you see how [Folly's] trying to show how far and foolishly Billie is willing to go to be in with the in-crowd? (Atwell 1987)

It's amazing to me how she [Judy Blume] can write a very serious book like Are You There God? It's Me, Margaret *and a funny book like* Freckle Juice. *I wonder where she gets her ideas from? (Story 1988)*

Why do you think Ramona wasn't so bad [in Ramona and Her Father*]? Do you think that Beverly Cleary just didn't make her as bad, or was there a reason within the book that made her act better? (Story 1988)*

QUESTIONS TO HELP READERS USE CUE SYSTEMS AND SELF-MONITORING STRATEGIES

Proficient readers use syntactic, semantic, and grapho-phonemic cues to predict what's coming next, narrow the alternatives, and confirm or correct their predictions (Smith, Goodman & Meredith 1970). Readers who are not accomplished in using a variety of combinations of cue systems, or who do not yet consistently self-monitor, need encouragement to develop fully these important strategies. Effective questions can do just that.

Teacher: Look at that. Look at the cover. I wonder what it's called?
Child: Astronauts.
Teacher: Well, it could be an astronaut, but does it start with *a*? (Wright Group 1987)

Child (silently rereading): I said "lizard" but its *lizard's.*
Teacher: How did you know?
Child: 'Cause it's got an *s.*
Teacher: Is there any other way we could know?
Child (re-runs): It's funny to say "lizard dinner"! It has to be "lizard's dinner," like Peter's dinner, doesn't it?
Teacher: Yes, that was good. You found two ways to check on that tricky new word. (Clay 1979a)

Teacher: What was that new word you read?
Child: Bicycle.
Teacher: How did you know it was *bicycle?*
Child: It was a bike.
Teacher: What else did you expect to see?
Child: A *b.*
Teacher: What else?
Child: A little word, but it wasn't.
Teacher: So what did you do?
Child: I thought of *bicycle.*
Teacher: Good, I liked the way you worked at that all by yourself. (Clay 1979a)

QUESTIONS TO SATISFY THE TEACHER'S CURIOSITY

Students are not the only ones who are inquisitive. Often teachers are curious, wondering about things for which they have no immediate an-

40

Rebecca Huntsman

swers. Those answers often lie with the students—if only we'd ask them. Atwell (1987) believes that students have the potential to teach teachers a great deal if given the opportunity. Calkins learned much about the writing process from talking to and questioning children who were writers. She wondered, "Is it the children who teach and we who learn?" (1983, p. 8).

I've been trying to think of a way to keep track of the best books our class reads, so that when someone finishes a book, they can find another good one easily. Do you have any ideas about how to do that? (Story 1988)

Kids here seem really interested in the past and they have taught me a lot. The kids at my last school weren't that interested. I wonder why they are so different? (Story 1988)

Response

Effective teachers use questions *and* response to teach. Through response, teachers can share with the reader their understanding of the reading process.

RESPONSE TO DEMONSTRATE READING IS FUNCTIONAL

Effective teachers communicate to students that print serves a purpose, that writing is meant to be read. These teachers read the sign giving directions for making popcorn as they make the popcorn. They read the daily lunch menu instead of simply posting it. Through an invitation board, these teachers—and, with encouragement, their students—extend written invitations to others to draw pictures of their favorite cartoon characters, write "All About Me" books, join a baseball league, or simply help.

Dear Students ages from 6–13,
If you would like to join in summer league baseball program meet me after School on Monday. Your teacher will give you a signor-up sheet before you go home today. Bring it back Monday if you can play.

> Robby Martin
>
> (Loughlin & Martin 1987)

I found out the wind can travel in all different directions and that wind can be helpful to people by pushing sailboats and spinning windmills. I couldn't find out what the difference is between a tornado and a hurricane. Does anyone know?

> *Susan B.*
>
> *(Loughlin & Martin 1987)*

I need halp plees.

> *Lynette*
>
> *(Loughlin & Martin 1987)*

Effective teachers read books to the class and expose students to a variety of forms of writing. At times, they may employ the shared book experience (Holdaway 1979) or guided reading, but whenever they read, they model good reading. Effective teachers encourage learners of all ages to write and care more about function than form on first drafts. This helps students understand that there is "one word written for one word spoken" and also that words are always written the same way (Cambourne & Turbill 1987).

RESPONSE TO DEMONSTRATE THAT READING IS EXCITING

The attitudes of teachers can greatly affect the attitudes of their students. It follows then that if teachers want their students to be excited about books and reading, the teachers must be excited and demonstrate their enthusiasm. Effective teachers create excitement about texts and actively become involved in the readings themselves.

Rebecca Huntsman

Mrs. O'Brian: Last week I said we'd have a nice surprise today. It's a brand new book, and it's going to be a really neat one! What kind of book is this?
Class: A read-together.
Mrs. O'Brian: I'm dying to read it with you. (Wright Group 1987)

The Indian in the Cupboard [Banks 1980] sounds like a great book! I want to read it, too. I think it's funny they were arguing about a skateboard, considering there were no skateboards in the Indian's time. I'm curious to learn more about their arguments. I love books with lots of conflict! (Story 1988)

RESPONSE TO DEMONSTRATE THAT READING
INVOLVES EXPERIMENTATION

Effective teachers value writing, no matter what form it takes or whose it is. They realize the connection between reading and writing, the necessity of using each to inform the other. Effective teachers also allow learners to experiment with their own writings. They therefore encourage them to use letters, drawings, and marks on paper to tell a story. Effective teachers also permit invented spelling and approximation in both reading and writing as students begin to understand the sound/symbol relationships in written language and can then read their own texts.

My feet take me evrewhair. My feet like to clime trees. (Gentry 1987)

At my house i have some dayeses they are flowrs they growe in the spreing i pike them in the spreing the rain mak the flowrs growe and in the somre they all droy up and more flowrs growe bak and they have naw levs and i peke them agan. (Weaver 1988)

Through their responses, teachers can share their acceptance of invented spelling and approximations while simultaneously demonstrating conventional forms of spelling and writing:

You have active feet, Dan. My feet used to like to climb trees, but I'm afraid they've gotten tired! (Gentry 1987)

Are daises your favorite flowers? Do you have other flowers near your house that you also like to pick? Sometimes flowers can really cheer people up, can't they? (Weaver 1988)

RESPONSE TO DEMONSTRATE THAT READING IS MULTIMODAL

Like learning, reading is a multimodal process; many ways of knowing transact in the making of meaning. Readers combine speaking, listening, reading, and writing with drama, music, art, math, or language in order to clarify their understandings (Harste, Woodward & Burke 1984). Effective teachers provide opportunities for this meaning making to occur in diverse ways. They allow the children to play with words, engage in art and dance, put stories into dramatic forms and act them out for others, talk with each other, put complex ideas in the form of charts or graphs, and visualize events in their minds. Extensions of reading in this manner assist children in making meaning from print.

Maggie and Michael, without being told, naturally combined reading and writing with art to derive meaning from print. Atwell (1987) speaks of Jeff, who, although older than Maggie and Michael, does the same. Teachers who, through their responses, encourage children to use various means of knowing and hypothesis testing will find that the children become involved in and excited about what they are reading.

Teacher: Then what happened [to the cow]?
Betsy: She was hanging on the roof.
Teacher: (sketches a house with a flat roof): Betsy, will you draw where . . . uh . . . where the cow was hanging?
(Betsy draws the cow hanging between the roof and the ground.) (Goodman, Watson & Burke 1987)

Would you like to illustrate your book on horses with the new paints? Please let me know if you would and I'll help you set them up. (Loughlin & Martin 1987)

Would you enjoy taking the part of the story that you liked the best and making a flannel board story based on it or act it out in mime? (Huntsman, June 1989, Personal Communication)

Since you are so talented in music, how would you like to put the poem to a tune? If you like, and if Susan agrees, perhaps, with her training in dance, she could prepare an interpretive dance to go along with your music and you could both present it to the class. That might really help us understand the emotions in the poem and the feelings that the poet might have been experiencing. (Huntsman, June 1989, Personal Communication)

You say you aren't sure how William was tricked out of his money? OK, let's put the information the author gives you into a chart and see. (Huntsman, June 1989, Personal Communication)

On the story box videotape (Wright Group 1987), Mrs. O'Brian asks, "How about occasionally you can do the action?" And so we see the children jump when she reads "jumping"; they dance when she reads "dancing"; they pretend to fly when she reads "flying." Painting, listening posts, and stimulating innovations are all part of her follow-up activities. *Mrs. Wishy-Washy* (Cowley & Melser 1980) becomes a class-written text,

Rebecca Huntsman

Mrs. Splishy-Sploshy, and *The Hungry Giant* (Cowley 1980) becomes *The Hungry Children.*

RESPONSE TO DEMONSTRATE THAT READING IS SOCIAL

Reading does not take place in isolation. There is a flow of ideas between readers and authors as the written word takes on meaning for the readers. In turn, readers interact with those around them as they share what they've read. Reading therefore becomes a social activity—one from which students continue to learn as ideas are shared. Consider young Maggie, who, even without the encouragement of a teacher, sought to share her understanding of the written word rather than keep it to herself. Effective teachers build on this natural desire to share. They promote small-group discussion of topics or books read, in which students can talk to each other about literature, language, and reading. They encourage peer interaction, thus promoting a social reliance. Students can be found reading in pairs or larger groups.

Who was it that was reading The Jack Tales *[Chase 1943]? Maybe you could get together and compare the stories after she has read some and see if they are similar. Let me know what you find out, please! (Story 1988)*

My brother is studying oceanography in California and does a lot of skin-diving. He has a lot of shark stories to tell. Would you be interested in writing a letter to him? I would write a letter of introduction to accompany your letter and I can promise he would write back. (Story 1988)

Atwell (1987) and Bartoli and Botel (1988) suggest numerous invitations for encouraging this social aspect of reading:

- How are you different now from when you started this book?
- What do you know or think about now that you didn't know or think about before you started this book?
- What would you like to ask the author, or someone in the group, about the book?
- Does this book remind you of any other literature you know?
- How did the author get you to think?
- How did the author get you to feel happy, scared, sad?
- Do you see any patterns—in the pictures or story?
- What would you like to share with us?

45

Questioning and Responding

- What stood out for you?
- Which character did you identify with? Why?

Of utmost importance to all types of questions that effective teachers ask and to all types of responses that effective teachers make is the belief that all individuals can read. Effective teachers have positive expectations for students, and their questions and responses communicate this belief. Effective teachers praise; they don't belittle. These teachers build on students' strengths while supporting and encouraging their risk-taking attempts. They encourage students to try things they haven't done before, to attempt words they think they don't know, or to write when they feel they can't spell or aren't neat enough.

Well, you read that very nicely. Give yourself a clap because that was really good. I'll give you one too. (Wright Group 1987)

You're doing nicely writing this letter. . . . If you make a mistake, you can cross it out. . . . You're doing well. (Harste, Woodward & Burke 1984)

The two parts you told me [about the book you are reading] were really funny, made me laugh out loud. You could do an excellent book talk and entice everyone else to read the book by telling the class those two parts. (Story 1988)

Oh, yes, you do [read and write well]. If your writing looked like ours, there would be no reason for you to be there [in the classroom]. You know we can read anything you write. (Harste, Woodward & Burke, 1984)

Effective teachers use a combination of questions and responses to support learners and to communicate their belief in them. These teachers focus on learners' strengths; they view the teachable moment as an opportunity to enrich the students' learning further. With supportive teachers, literate environments, and positive expectations, students won't disappoint their teachers or themselves—they will read and, in the process, "outgrow their former selves" (Harste 1984).

what matters?

IT MATTERS THAT TEACHERS ESTABLISH
LEARNING-CENTERED ENVIRONMENTS

five

GETTING STARTED
Creating a Literate Classroom Environment
Noel K. Jones

If we assume that reading and writing are critical, reflective, personal processes and at the same time communicative and social experiences, and if we assume further that what matters in the long run is what matters every day, we will then understand the teacher's primary consideration to be: How do I get my students absorbed in meaningful reading and writing activities?

There are several advantages to starting with this question. One is that it is natural. In our culture, life situations automatically occur that engage people as communicators through reading and writing. If students find genuine purposes for literate communication at school, then they will perceive the connection between their learning and real life; they will more easily appreciate the importance of becoming literate. A second reason for starting with decisions that foster purposeful communications is that this orientation gives students responsibility for their own learning. The message—spoken or unspoken—that students' motives, purposes, interests, and strategies matter invites them to accept this responsibility whenever they feel that it is safe and important to do so. In urging movement in this direction, we are assuming that there is an essential difference between authentic or meaningful learning, which becomes part of the being of the student, and the limited, artificial learning that is typical of much traditional schooling—for example, the math computational skills we seldom use, or the smattering of foreign language or history or English grammar so many of us have memorized and forgotten.

The Problem of Change

Getting students absorbed in meaningful, purposeful literacy activities requires a number of significant changes in the classroom—in the physical environment, in events and activities, and in the nature and quality of interactions. It would be easy, albeit unrealistic (and also somewhat disconcerting), if teachers could snap their fingers and change everything that needs to be altered at once. But it is more realistic to begin by making just one or two changes, guided perhaps by a compelling goal or ideal, by a general concern about student performance, or by the influence of a mentor or friend. There is usually a gradual progression in initiating change and, as change occurs, sometimes the original aim or intent shifts in emphasis. As John Dewey (1916) noted, goals serve as "ends-in-view"; they may never actually be realized, but they guide the actions and decisions of the practitioner, and they themselves change along the way.

A teacher may begin, for example, with the goal of getting students to enjoy reading more. Moving in that direction, she or he may decide that the basal reader and current teaching practices are getting in the way and she or he may try out some form of self-selected reading. Now she or he becomes concerned with getting students to be more critical and involved with what they read. This concern motivates and guides other innovations.

When attempting to make changes toward purposeful reading activities, toward a literate environment, it may help for teachers to keep two things in mind. First, they should not be put off by the degree of difference between their current situation and the ideas and practices discussed in this volume. You *can* get there from here. We all did, really, though perhaps some of us were fortunate in starting out in a situation in which a high degree of literacy was going on. Second, teachers should keep in mind that the suggestions we offer are only guidelines, not specific recommendations for action. Our intent is not to prescribe an agenda for change. Teachers need to decide what to do in their own situations and with their own students.

The Classroom Environment

In making changes in the physical aspects of the classroom, the ultimate aim is to create an environment that supports, facilitates, and invites literacy—an environment filled with messages received, messages sent, messages shared, and invitations to send messages. There are, however, no formulas or rules to follow in structuring the physical dimensions of literate environments. They have been developed in almost every kind of condition, from the natural "classrooms" of outdoor education, to carpeted, well-equipped, modern schoolrooms. Decisions need to be made about choice and arrangement of furniture, use of space, selection of materials, and provisions for their use. We offer the following guidelines:

1. Each aspect of the physical environment should invite and facilitate literate activities. For example, chairs for reading or browsing should be comfortable, not forbidding; and print materials and writing paraphernalia should not just *be* in the classroom, they should be invitingly displayed.
2. Places for undisturbed reading and writing should be available, as

well as places for conversation and sharing of ideas. If different areas aren't available, furniture can be rearranged at times, or different rules and guidelines may operate from one time to another.

3. The environment should reflect and provide evidence of literate activities. Teachers should create space for displays of authentic messages of all kinds: individual mailboxes for personal messages, a message board for public announcements and invitations, posters advertising important events or a book that a child has read, displays of stories and poems and published books by student authors . . . the list could go on and on.

4. Students should be encouraged to share ownership of the classroom environment and the literacy materials and messages it contains. They should be allowed to make decisions about the environment and the rules and procedures for its use. And they should do as much of the work, and assume as much of the responsibility, as they are capable of doing.

5. Teachers should be concerned with the symbolism of the environment, as well as with its functional aspects. Many subtle symbols within a classroom signal whether authentic communication is valued. A teacher desk at the front of the room, chalkboards and bulletin boards reserved only for the teacher's use, or constraints on access to books and materials, tell students that they are really playing a game for which someone else has written the rules. In contrast, books invitingly displayed, signs and seating identifying conference areas, and notices inviting written responses all signify that children are expected and welcome to send and receive messages about subjects over which they have some choice.

Events and Activities

In a literate environment, events and activities serve three functions: they encourage students to send, receive, and share genuine messages; they allow the teacher and other learners to demonstrate literate abilities; and they provide content or topics for communication. In order for this to occur, literacy activities must have a major share of the daily routine of the classroom. Reading corners or writing centers are of little use if children aren't given opportunity to use them; and writing as homework or communication only at recess makes little contribution to the development of critical literacy. Time and opportunity alone are not enough, however; teachers must initiate and foster a range of communication and literacy experiences. Not only must print materials of all kinds be in the classroom, but teachers must also treat them as messages, by reading aloud to students from the books, by talking about authors and communicating with authors, by showing students that they themselves are frequently senders and receivers of interesting written messages, by sending personal written messages to children (messages that are *not* in some way mechanisms for control), by inviting students to return messages, and by encouraging and supporting the exchange of messages among students.

The realization that young readers and writers use strategies for which they gradually develop working concepts and rules lends greater emphasis to the role of demonstrations in acquiring literacy than was previously acknowledged. Demonstrations of communication roles, styles, and processes by teachers and other students serves as an important learning resource in the classroom. When a teacher and his (or her) students write together and read together, everyone involved profits.

Both regular and special classroom activities can serve as content or stimulate interesting ideas for student communication. Teachers must be alert to every opportunity to relate classroom communications to people, events, and activities within and beyond the classroom's walls. Corresponding with people or organizations at a distance, inviting people into the school, and taking field trips provide excellent opportunities and purposes for many kinds of oral and written communication. Teachers can create communication opportunities within the classroom by fostering small-group activities and projects. Science experiments, social studies projects, mathematical problems, peer editing or reaction to compositions, and all kinds of responses to literature (dramatizations, stories, choral readings, etc.) are possible group activities that provide purposes for, or flow from, reading and writing experiences. Other activities or events less directly related to the traditional curriculum—such as a classroom newspaper, interest groups, and special projects—may also serve such purposes. In addition to the above suggestions, the following guidelines may be helpful:

1. Teachers should capitalize upon student experience and areas of interest to provide content for literacy activities. They can begin by asking children what their interests are.
2. Materials should be available on topics that typically interest children of the appropriate age. Dinosaurs, folktales, and animal stories are

Noel K. Jones

usually sure-fire winners. Generally, the more that learners have a share in controlling the content of activities, the better.

3. Students should have opportunities to browse and to explore a topic in depth.
4. Teachers should demonstrate for students—both deliberately and incidentally—learning and inquiry strategies, communication roles and styles, and writing and communication processes.
5. Teachers should devise as many opportunities as possible for students to communicate and share ideas, information, and questions. If a child comments that other children leave the art corner messy, a teacher might suggest that the child compose a poster to remind others to clean up. One child in the Ed Lab, after discussing with his tutor the extinction of dinosaurs, decided to take a written survey to see if other people agreed with his conclusions.
6. Teachers should maintain a low profile in supplying and fostering the purpose and content of communications. The teacher is and should be an important person within the classroom, but the test of appropriateness of teacher's decisions on events and activities is the degree to which students become excited about and accept responsibility for their own learning. For this to happen the teacher needs to avoid attention while exerting influence in subtle ways.

Interactions

Whereas events and activities within the classroom establish the content and purposes for literacy, interactions support the processes of literacy: learners develop their abilities as readers and writers largely through interaction with teachers and/or other students. Two different kinds of interactions that need to be considered are (1) cycles of involvement in literacy activities, and (2) response to readers and writers at various stages within those cycles of involvement.

Both reading and writing proceed through cycles involving *preparation* (pre-writing or pre-reading), *engagement* (drafting or reading), *revisitation* (revision or rereading), and *sharing*. The beginnings and the ends, and frequently the revisitations, of these cycles are grounded in social concerns and interactions. We begin to write with an audience in mind, even though we may not be conscious of the audience we intend. Purposes for reading are also socially grounded; we read with an awareness of authors as persons or with an awareness of the application of what we

Getting Started

are reading to social contexts or to personal concerns that are socially influenced. Even if we tear up a hateful letter we just wrote, our decision not to share what we had put into words has both a social motivation and an effect on our relations with others. Although we frequently remain silent after reading an article or book, the experience may influence other communication experiences directly or in subtle ways. Certainly the urge to tell about an interesting book or article is common and quite natural. Sharing ideas with others after reading can clarify, authenticate, extend, reevaluate, and allow us to apply meanings. The essential point, however, is that the meaning of what we read is socially influenced. We frequently seek confirmation from others of our interpretations of what we read.

It follows then that if classroom literacy experiences are to be critical, reflective, and part of authentic learning experiences, they must be grounded in social interactions in the classroom and school. These interactions may include the on-going, communal activities that make up the life of the classroom as well as special events and activities initiated by the teacher, by students, or by other people within or outside the school. If students are given considerable choice in what they read and write about, these communal experiences will naturally serve as preparation for some literacy activities and as revisitation and sharing for others. Teachers can further ensure that pupil-to-pupil interactions take place by structuring and fostering group processes within the classroom. In a truly literate environment people work together in groups for any number of reasons; such work may even entail the most intense intellectual engagement of their lives. Group interaction of this type can, and should be, part of the classroom environment. Beginning to use groups is not always easy—it requires some planning and preparation—but the benefits are tremendous.

Response to messages occurs readily in most natural communication situations. In a classroom functioning as a literate environment students will have many opportunities to share with their classmates the things they are interested in—such as messages received, projects, plans, objects of affection, and so forth. In addition, the teacher needs to respond in subtle and supportive ways, to encourage students to reflect upon their own abilities as readers and writers.

Responses that foster reflection can come in group situations or in dyadic (one-to-one) interaction, from other students or from the teacher. Such response can occur at any point in the cycle of literacy experiences. At the preparation stage, response from a group, or an individual, can suggest or help focus ideas for exploration and strategies for selecting books or topics for writing. For example, during October when students get a chance to create their own jack-o'-lantern faces and write about Halloween, their excited comments about "What *I'm* gonna make" or "What *I'm* gonna write" stimulate inventive variation and reveal a range of options.

At the engagement stage, response from another person, and at the revisitation stage, response from a group or from an individual, may cause students to reflect on their strategies and literate abilities as well as the meanings of messages. Examples of responses might include a student reading aloud to a teacher, a teacher replying to a young writer's question about a topic or about spelling, student groups discussing how to enact a story or figuring out the meaning of a science article; a teacher holding individual conferences with students to discuss reading selections or the revision of compositions; and a group of students responding to each other's compositions in a writing workshop. Individual or group response may also occur during the sharing stage: a teacher's response to students' journal entries; a student's written response to another student's composition; class discussion or panel discussion of a story or book read by some or all students; group response to the choral reading renditions of a group or the entire class; and responses from classmates after students have read compositions aloud.

At any one of these stages, response serves an evaluative function, but evaluative judgements should not be externally imposed. Response should allow students to judge the effectiveness of their own communications and the validity of their own ideas and information. At the same time, however, response increases awareness of their strategies and accomplishments, makes them feel good about themselves as learners, and encourages them to attempt new strategies and forms of expression.

Teachers should be skilled in responding to learners in ways that foster critical reflection and in helping students respond effectively to one another. The following guidelines may be helpful:

1. Teachers should respond genuinely to the meaning and intent of the child's messages. Too often, we say "That's nice" and proceed to criticize the child's form or method of communication, or impose value judgments. Communication dries up if messages do not receive meaningful and genuine response.
2. Teachers should call attention to reading and writing processes at the

Getting Started

engagement and revisitation stages by suggesting or confirming appropriate strategies (e.g., "You knew that word couldn't be _____ so you went back and changed it. How did you know that?" or "If that word was _____, what would it look like?"). Response of this type is helpful when students are developing strategies, as signaled by their hesitations, searching behaviors, or self-corrections. But responses must be both well timed and minimal. (Less is probably better!)

3. Students should be given the right to judge themselves as readers and writers. Teacher and student responses to the meaning and intent of communications provide a basis for children to make such judgments; however, teachers' questions and comments also help the students become aware of the effectiveness of their communications. Fostering awareness, without divesting students of the right to evaluate themselves, is not easy, as there are many subtle ways to impose judgments on learners.

Teachers must guide students to respond to one another in helpful ways; learners should learn to (a) accept the obligation to respond to communications directed at them; (b) recognize the value of others' opinions as well as their right to express themselves; (c) respect other students as individuals, without imposing judgment; (d) not let concern for others' opinions or reactions prevent them from expressing their own ideas and beliefs; (e) listen to what the other person is communicating, rather than jumping to conclusions; and (f) be helpful to other students as learners and as emerging readers and writers. (In other words, teachers should stress cooperation rather than competition.)

Noel K. Jones

Suggestions for Getting Started

By this time, it should be apparent that the authors of this volume are offering no recipes or sure steps for developing higher levels of literacy in any particular environment. It should also be apparent that we feel much the same way about the professional development of teachers as we do about the development of literacy in children. Motivation for growth and the direction of growth are the responsibility of the individual teacher/learner (in a literate environment, all teachers are learners and all learners are teachers), although any learner can certainly be influenced and supported by a "significant other." What we recommend is a cycle of *reflection, planning, action,* and *observation,* which may begin with any one of these stages and continue indefinitely. The method has been variously called "inquiry," "action research," and "critical praxis" (Goswami and Stillman 1987; Strickland 1988).

Teachers may begin by *observing* their own classrooms, including their students and themselves, to judge the extent to which a literate environment exists. *Reflection* might focus on such questions as "I wonder why my students dislike writing?" "What would happen if I didn't grade compositions, but introduced ways of sharing instead?" and "What would I most like to change about my own performance and/or the performance of my students?" At this point a decision should be made to *plan* a specific change and *to take action* to put that plan into effect. *Observation* of the process and of the results comes next, followed by *reflection* on what happened. This leads to tentative explanations and hypotheses, then further *plans, actions,* and *observations.*

What is suggested is not an easy process. Many teachers have been trained to expect that teaching is primarily a matter of following established paths. Others are directed, or feel pressured by accountability systems, to teach prescribed objectives or to teach within a specific style. Launching out on one's own as an educational innovator can be risky, frightening, and difficult. There are ways of making this decision a little easier. First, teachers should enlist support. If at all possible, they should find someone with whom they can talk freely. This person may serve as confidant or sounding board, or may even spend time in the classroom as an observer, sharing perceptions of what is happening. The confidant may be a fellow teacher, a parent, a friend, a relative or spouse, a supervisor, principal, or university instructor. Teachers still carry all the responsibility for decision-making within the classroom, but having someone to talk to reduces this burden considerably.

A second suggestion is for teachers to write about what they are doing. Writing stimulates the flow of ideas and helps us collect, sort, and evaluate our thoughts. It also provides a record of progress. Teachers may be surprised at the insights about students, about themselves, and about schools generated through the practice of thoughtful writing. Writing is not suggested in lieu of, but in addition to, a confidant. It is especially useful for teachers to share what they write with their professional friends.

Finally, teachers might consider taking their students into confidence and discussing with them what they are attempting to do and their reactions to it. Taking this step may make things easier, and it establishes a precedent of valuing students' ideas, treating students as people we trust and consider responsible. This step symbolizes one of the most important changes teachers want to make—a change in the role of learner and in the relationships between teacher and learners in the classroom.

Impediments to Change

Students attitudes and expectations sometimes make change difficult. Good students are accustomed to being rewarded for competitive, individual achievement, while poor students find release from obligation by being perceived as failures. Therefore, many students are quite satisfied to treat school as a comfortable, predictable game. Real learning, on the other hand, can be frustrating, hard work, so students may be both with and against teachers as they initiate change.

Textbooks, curriculum guides, standardized tests, and the expectations of administrators and community members also impede change. This serious, complex issue cannot receive adequate treatment here, but I would like to offer a few comments.

First of all, there is a very strong movement and tradition supporting the approach to literacy education advocated here. The forces that support training on isolated skills (with accompanying emphasis on prescribed programs, criterion and standardized testing, and teacher accountability) may be dominant in your school system or region and may be in the majority nationwide. The counter-movement is strong, however, among theorists, teacher trainers, and teachers and seems to be gaining strength against the technological interests. There is a great deal of ideational, practical, and political support for the positions outlined here.

Second, curriculum expectations are seldom as rigid as they appear to the classroom practitioner. Curriculum pathways and instructional programs are justified in terms of more general educational goals. Most educators and lay persons will agree with the goal of critical, reflective literacy as defined in this volume; their arguments will be concerned with methods of achieving that goal. If teachers can demonstrate results—students functioning well as readers and writers according to usual expectations of age and grade—they will certainly have a very strong claim to legitimacy of method toward an accepted long-range goal. Remember also, that even in systems that try to prescribe programs, and pacing

58

Noel K. Jones

within those programs, teachers play a large role in determining the curriculum within their own classrooms. A teacher can continue to use the basal reader or other adopted textbooks and still make a number of changes in the directions suggested in this volume.

Third, teachers should remember that the best way to achieve a high level of literacy in the long run is to engage in thoughtful, communicative literacy on a daily basis. Our national educational results hardly justify continuation of a skills-centered, instrumental approach. Even American college graduates are widely criticized for their lack of interest and comprehension in reading and for the poor quality of their written compositions. On the other hand, children in schools that take very seriously the creation of literate environments regularly demonstrate a wide range of communication skills. The kinds of interactions, events, and activities discussed in this volume *will* produce children who can perform well on any measure of literacy including achievement tests.

Fourth, teachers must anticipate questions and criticisms about their approach. The most convincing arguments for what they are doing are students who are excited about reading, writing, and learning and who regularly function consistently as readers and writers compared to developmental expectations. Not everyone can visit the classroom to see students in action. Therefore, teachers must systematically collect evidence of the literate abilities of their students. Teachers should maintain writing folders for each child, and keep published books, charts, posters, reports, and other samples of work. Children can keep records of books they have read; oral reading performance can be taped at beginning, middle, and end of the year. Of course, the most convincing evidence for parents is the reading and writing that children choose to do at home. If teachers develop in their classroom real enthusiasm for writing, reading, and literature, and if they allow time for writing and reading in school and encourage independent exploration of new learning, the spillover to homes and families will be both unavoidable and impressive.

Finally, as teachers embark on a process of change and reflect on their experiences and observations as teachers and learners, they should think critically about those customary practices and beliefs that appear as impediments to change. Whom do they benefit? Whose purposes are being served by publicizing standardized test scores? By using the basal reader? By expecting all teachers to proceed through materials at the same pace? By imposing statewide or systemwide curriculum expectations? By attempts to make instructional programs "teacher-proof"? If the answer to each of these questions is not "learners," then something is wrong. We have discovered perhaps the most compelling reason for getting started with changes that foster the establishment of a literate environment in the classroom.

60

Noel K. Jones

what matters?

IT MATTERS THAT TEACHERS CONTINUALLY REFLECT

six

TOUCHSTONES FOR TEACHING
Jennifer Story

It is August 15. After picking up your key from the office, you chat for a while with the other teachers, then head out to your classroom. Opening the door, you feel a little overwhelmed. The room is much the same as you left it—except that the floor has been waxed and a set of bookshelves built approximately where you asked for them.

But the same old desks are piled against the wall. In the coat closet, covered with dusty yellow craft paper, are the basal readers, one set for below-grade level, a set for on-grade level, and a set for above-grade level. Who knows how many you'll have assigned to each reading group this year?

The ideas described in the preceding chapters are stirring, but the old "what to do on Monday morning" dilemma can be daunting. It is hard to imagine how to organize around these ideals when you are faced with a class of twenty-five to thirty kids, and only one or two adults. But it can be done.

In my own classroom, it helps to have touchstones with which to gauge my practices. The art of teaching is so fluid, so unpredictable, and offers so many possible directions for learning, that I can't keep everything I know about teaching at the forefront of my mind to guide my decision making. So I try to distill my ideals of teaching to as few as possible so I can get a grasp on them.

Touchstone 1: Learning Is Natural

Frank Smith describes seven characteristics of the learning that takes place as young children accomplish the monumental task of learning to talk: "The learning is always (1) meaningful, (2) useful, (3) continual and effortless, (4) incidental, (5) collaborative, (6) vicarious, and (7) free of risk" (1988, 6). One of my roles as a teacher is to maintain a learning environment that will assist children to learn "school subjects" as naturally as they learned to talk. When I find myself taking too much control of the learning, doing what administrators or other teachers think I ought to be doing, I mentally finger my "natural" touchstone and realign my practices with my beliefs.

The story of the yo-yo men serves as a good example of learning in a natural environment. When yo-yos experienced a revival of interest, fifth graders Steve, LaMont, and Carter began learning all the tricks. They called themselves "the yo-yo men" and decided to write a book describing yo-yo tricks. I was pleased with their choice of a project and with their decision to work together. Steve had a hard time finding a lasting interest; LaMont did whatever he thought he was supposed to do, but had a problem communicating clearly in writing; and Carter was a talented writer and self-starter, who could act as an organizing force in the group. Every day during writing class, the three went to the end of one of the halls where they wouldn't disturb anyone, and two of them yo-yoed while one wrote. Together, they tried to accomplish the difficult task of transposing actions into words.

It's easy to see how most of the characteristics of learning that Smith describes are functioning in this event. Writing a book of yo-yo tricks was meaningful and useful to these boys. In an incidental fashion, they were learning the academic subjects of spelling, grammar, punctuation, organization, and coherent writing. The learning was effortless to them and continual. The learning was also collaborative, as each boy brought a different world of knowledge and expertise to the task, and as I helped them solve problems and periodically reviewed their work, making suggestions and later helping them edit and publish.

The initial writing was free of risk because there was no one to tell them they were wrong, but so was the stage where I intervened. The structure of writing workshop does not include a judgmental phase at which one can fail. When the teacher helps with the revising or editing stages by pointing out a sentence that is not clear or showing the students the rule for plurals of words that end in *f,* students receive the help. There is no threat and students are spared the discouraging messages sent by a red "awk" on the final draft of a theme paper or by a failing score on a spelling test.

The learning these "yo-yo men" absorbed was tremendous, but I couldn't possibly have written behavioral objectives that would have predicted what they would learn. To have tried to do so would have put a limit on what I would allow them to learn as I tried to push them in the direction I thought they should go.

I have often felt pressure from my school system to change, to conform to the ways others teach. At times, this pressure has been direct and, at other times, it comes from my own uncertainty. Sometimes my faith in myself falters because I am very much alone in my region with my philosophy. It is then that my touchstones become vital. When I compare the characteristics of natural learning with the work metaphor that traditionally characterizes schooling, I regain my confidence.

Jennifer Story

LEARNING IS NATURAL	LEARNING IS WORK
Meaningful and useful	*Prescribed*
Continual and effortless	*Programmed for difficulty*
Incidental and vicarious	*Controlled*
Collaborative	*Competitive*
Free of risk	*Evaluative*

Touchstone 2: Learners Are Apprentices

During the 87–88 school year, I implemented reading workshop for teaching reading and writing workshop for language classes; in doing so, I came closer to my ideal of being a facilitator of learning. In the style of teaching described by Nancy Atwell (1987), the children wrote during their language arts period, and read books of their choice and wrote in dialogue journals during reading class. When I first began my classes this way, I was not entirely certain what my role would be. I had set up the conditions for a natural learning environment and knew I would provide guidance in making choices and assist students as they used language and conventions, but I didn't really have a grasp of what I would be doing at any given moment. It was very different from the six-step lesson plan I had been drilled in—to start with anticipatory set and end with closure.

The reading and writing workshops actually went rather smoothly, and I found the kids defined my role for me—giving me another touchstone to define and refine my teaching. I discovered we were working together in a master-apprentice relationship, in which they learned the crafts of reading and writing through trying them and I guided their learning as a master silversmith assists his apprentices. I read with them, wrote with them, and advised them as we all moved toward our vision of excellence.

Touchstone 3: Teaching as Parenting

On an individual basis, my role is to act more like a parent toward learners in the same way I enjoy reading with my three-year-old daughter. I'm not trying to teach her to read at three; I'm participating in an activity we both love, and it so happens that she is learning voraciously. If I acted like a teacher and required her to identify letters, to tell me stories she already knows, asked her comprehension questions, or tried to turn her answers back on her to make her think about the answers instead of freely following her interests and leads, she would soon come to dislike reading and would refuse to participate.

In the same way, I try to be a parent to my students as I guide their learning. I try to discover as much as I can about the individual children, what they already know, what their interests are, their dislikes, their strengths, and their needs. Then I can help to make their learning as effortless as possible. Because I know that fifth-grader Duane is writing on the level of a second grader, I express unrestrained delight when he shares his first personal experience story—a far cry from the short captions that he had been using to label his sequenced illustrations. And I definitely won't suggest he revise his story, something many other fifth graders do as a matter of choice. I'll suspect Duane might be ready to think about revision the first time he writes something he's not totally satisfied with.

Just as a parent treats a teenager and toddler differently according to their needs, my role in helping fifth-grader Buck is completely different. He is a very capable writer working with two friends on the script for a "splatter flick," a conglomeration of all the bloodiest movies they have ever seen. In the course of informal conferences with the group, we discuss the differences between writing a narrative and a script and the format for writing a script. Buck thinks the script is so good that the local movie studio would be interested in buying it. I help him find the studio's address and we break out the language textbook to find the model of a business letter. Not wanting to sound like an elementary school student, Buck rewrites and rereads his letter until he has achieved the mature voice he is seeking. With the letter in the mail and the script finished, the triumvirate breaks up. By the time the studio replies (they did not want to buy the script), Buck is writing his version of the *Guinness Book of World Records* and the other two are constructing props for a puppet show, their dreams of fame and fortune laid aside.

It is not always easy to operate within this "teacher as parent" role.

Jennifer Story

One of the hardest situations for me is deciding what to do when a child seems not to be growing.

In the first semester of writing workshop, Ray was writing short, bare, narrative pieces, one after the other, and all very similar. They all began, "Once there was a boy..." and, in half a page, the boy got into impossible situations and got out again by equally impossible means. Ray showed little interest in editing or publishing his work and, since writing workshop was experimental for me, his lack of growth made me nervous. I began making various suggestions for improving Ray's future pieces, but he continued writing story after story with no alterations in his formula. At about the same time as I started to consider forcing Ray to try some different techniques, he announced in reading workshop that he had read all the nonfiction animal books in the library that interested him and there was nothing more to read. His mother and I tried to lure him into different kinds of books. Finally, his mother succeeded in interesting him in Jim Kjielgard's novels, *Big Red, Stormy,* and others. One day in writing workshop, he wrote a long story, completely different from his little tales about the boy. His new writing contained descriptions of the characters, animals, and detailed images of the action. In one day, he had taken a giant leap into mature writing. He now wanted to publish his work, so he was willing to work with me as I helped him with spelling and punctuation. On subsequent pieces he was interested in listening to what other writers suggested for his work.

What I learned from Ray, and from many other students who passed through a plateau in their learning growth, was that I needed to be very patient and trusting. I learned to trust that the apprentices were really there to learn the trade, that they really wanted to read and write. I also learned to trust myself and my faith that learning should be natural and, even when I couldn't see the learning that was occurring, to believe that if children are interested in what they are doing, they are learning from it.

On the other hand, I had to learn to trust my instincts enough to sense the difference between a child who was on a plateau and one who was bogged down, continually writing the same sort of piece, perhaps out of fear of trying something new. A child trapped into repetition needed my careful intervention to find directions to grow that were not threatening. Without textbooks making decisions for me and having to rely so much on myself, I needed my touchstones to assure myself that my decisions were the appropriate ones.

Touchstones for
Teaching

My touchstones guide all my decision making. When planning the semester or the next day, I am aware of whether I am stepping outside my guidelines of keeping learning natural. And as I make thousands of decisions each day in responding to individuals, I remember my parent-learner role. When I set up conditions for learning in my whole classroom, I keep in mind that I am organizing a learners' guild, an association of individuals with similar goals who learn by trying and who learn from each other and from me. And, above all, I try to remember to trust the apprentices, the learners, to believe in them and their acceptance of responsibility, to remember that we are pursuing a common goal of becoming better readers, writers, and informed citizens.

Jennifer Story

afterword

Janine Toomes, Jennifer Story, Rebecca Huntsman, and Donna Lindquist are all teachers who completed a Master's degree at the University of North Carolina at Wilmington. Noel Jones is a professor in the School of Education there. Diane Stephens was on the faculty from 1986–1988, and during that time she developed and directed the Educational Laboratory (Ed Lab). She also taught undergraduate and graduate courses.

The Ed Lab was and is a part of the teacher education program at the University of North Carolina at Wilmington (UNC-W). It provides pre- and in-service teachers with a supervised practicum experience, is transdisciplinary, and is associated with methods courses in reading, elementary, and special education.

This book was both collaborative and generative. As we wrote and rewrote, revised and edited, we learned about writing, about teaching, and most importantly, about learning. Together, we became a learners' guild. We carry lessons from our guild with us as memory, as strategy, as response, as curriculum: Jennifer Story is now education director at the Bishop Museum in Honolulu, Hawaii; Janine Toomes and Donna Lindquist teach methods courses and supervise student teachers at UNC-W; Rebecca Hunt teaches English and composition courses at Miller Mott Business College; Joan Gillette works with adult non-readers; Noel Jones is spending a year in Ohio being trained as a reading recovery teacher/leader and will return to UNC-W in the fall; and Diane Stephens conducts research at the Center for the Study of Reading and teaches classes for the College of Education, University of Illinois.

works cited

Atwell, N. 1987. *In the middle.* Portsmouth, NH: Boynton/Cook.

Bailey, J., P. Brazee, S. Chiavaroli, J. Herbeck, T. Lechner, A. McKittrick, L. Redwine, K. Reid, B. Robinson, and H. Spear. 1988. Problem solving our way to alternative evaluation procedure. *Language Arts* 65: 364–73.

Banks, L. 1980. *The Indian in the cupboard.* New York: Doubleday.

Bartoli, J., and M. Botel. 1988. *Reading/learning disability: An ecological approach.* New York: Teachers College Press.

Bissex, G. 1980. Patterns of development in writing: A case study. *Theory in Practice* 19: 197–201.

Blume, J. 1974. *The pain and the great one.* Scarsdale, NY: Bradbury Press.

Burke, C. 1985. Written conversations. In *The authoring cycle: A viewing guide,* ed. J. C. Harste, K. Pierce, and T. Cairney. Portsmouth, NH: Heinemann.

Bussis, A. 1982. "Burn it at the casket": Research, reading instruction, and children's learning of the first R. *Phi Delta Kappan* 64: 237–41.

Calkins, L. 1983. *Lessons from a child.* Portsmouth, NH: Heinemann.

Cambourne, B. 1984. Language, learning, and literacy. In *Towards a reading-writing classroom,* ed. A. Butler and J. Turbill. Portsmouth, NH: Heinemann.

Cambourne, B., and J. Turbill. 1987. *Coping with chaos.* Rozelle, New South Wales: Primary English Teaching Association. Distributed in the U.S. by Heinemann.

Carroll, L. 1866. *Alice's adventures in wonderland.* New York: Macmillan.

Chall, J. 1983. *Stages of reading development.* New York: McGraw-Hill.

Chase, R. 1943. *The Jack tales.* Boston: Houghton Mifflin.

Chomsky, N. 1965. *Aspects of the theory of syntax.* Cambridge, MA: MIT Press.

Christopher, M. 1979. *Dirt bike racer.* Boston: Little, Brown.

Clark, M. 1984. Literacy at home and at school: Insights from a study of young fluent readers. In *Awakening to Literacy,* ed. H. Goelman, A. Oberg, and F. Smith, 122–30. Portsmouth, NH: Heinemann.

Clay, M. 1975. *What did I write?* Portsmouth, NH: Heinemann.

———. 1977. Exploring with a pencil. *Theory into Practice* 16: 334–41.

———. 1979a. *The early detection of reading difficulties.* (2nd edition). Portsmouth, NH: Heinemann.

———. 1979b. *The patterning of complex behavior.* Portsmouth, NH: Heinemann.

Cohen, E. 1986. *Designing groupwork: Strategies for the heterogeneous classroom.* New York: Teachers College Press.

Cole, J. 1983. *Cars and how they go.* New York: Harper & Row.

Cowley, J. 1980. *The hungry giant.* Auckland, New Zealand: Shortland Publication Ltd.

Cowley, J., and J. Melser. 1980. *Mrs. Wishy-Washy.* Auckland, New Zealand: Shortland Publication Ltd.

Dewey, J. 1916. *Democracy and education.* New York: Macmillan.

Doake, D. 1985. Reading-like behavior: Its role in learning to read. In Jagger and Smith-Burke, 1985, 82–98.

Durkin, D. 1966. *Children who read early.* New York: Teachers College Press.

Eastman, P. D. 1973. *Big dog . . . little dog.* New York: Random House.

Ferreiro, E., and A. Teberosky. 1982. *Literacy before schooling.* Portsmouth, NH: Heinemann.

Genishi, C., A. McCarrier, and N. R. Nussbaum. 1988. Research currents: Dialogue as a context for teaching and learning. *Language Arts* 65: 184–91.

Gentry, R. 1987. *Spel . . . is a four-letter word.* Portsmouth, NH: Heinemann.

Goodman, K. 1976. Reading: A psycholinguistic guessing game. *Journal of the Reading Specialist* 6: 126–35.

———. 1977. Acquiring literacy is natural: Who skilled cock robin? *Theory into Practice* 16: 309–14.

Goodman, K., and Y. Goodman. 1979. Learning to read is natural. In *Theory and practice of early reading,* ed. L. B. Resnick and P. A. Weaver. Hillsdale, NJ: Erlbaum.

Goodman, Y. 1978. Kidwatching: An alternative to testing. *National Elementary Principal* 57: 41–45.

———. 1984. The development of initial literacy. In *Awakening to Literacy,* ed. H. Goelman, A. Oberg, and F. Smith. Portsmouth, NH: Heinemann.

———. 1985. Kidwatching: Observing children in the classroom. In Jagger and Smith-Burke 1985, 9–18.

Goodman, Y., V. A. Watson, and C. L. Burke. 1987. *Reading miscue inventory:* Alternate procedure. New York: Richard C. Owen.

Goswami, D., and P. Stillman. 1987. *Reclaiming the classroom: Teacher research as an agency for change.* Portsmouth, NH: Boynton/Cook.

Halliday, M. 1973. Three aspects of children's language development:

Learning language, learning through language, learning about language. Mimeograph.

Harp, B. 1988. When the principal asks: "When you do whole language instruction, how will you keep track of reading and writing skills?" *The Reading Teacher* 42: 160–61.

Harste, J. 1984. Personal communication.

Harste, J., V. Woodward, and C. Burke. 1984. *Language stories and literacy lessons.* Portsmouth, NH: Heinemann.

Hill, Eric. 1980. *Where's Spot?* New York: Putnam.

Holdaway, D. 1979. *The foundations of literacy.* Portsmouth, NH: Heinemann.

Jagger, A. 1985. On Observing the language learner: Introduction and overview. Jagger and Smith-Burke 1985, 1–7.

Jagger, A., and M. T. Smith-Burke. 1985. *Observing the language learner.* Newark, DE: International Reading Association.

Johnson, P. 1987. Steps toward a more naturalistic approach to the assessment of the reading process. In *Advances in context-based educational assessment,* ed. J. Algina. Norwood, NJ: Ablex.

Lindquist, D. 1988. Joining the literacy club. *The Reading Teacher* 41: 676–80.

Loughlin, C., and M. Martin. 1987. *Supporting literacy.* New York: Teachers College Press.

McKenzie, M. 1986. *Journeys into literacy.* Huddersfield, England: Schofield and Sims Ltd.

Minns, H. 1988. Teacher inquiry in the classroom: "Read it to me now!" *Language Arts* 65: 403–09.

Newman, J. 1984. *The craft of children's writing.* Portsmouth, NH: Heinemann.

———. 1985. *Whole language: theory in use.* Portsmouth, NH: Heinemann.

Rhodes, L. K., and C. Dudley-Marling. 1988. *Readers and writers with a difference.* Portsmouth, NH: Heinemann.

Rosenblatt, L. M. 1978. *The reader, the text, the poem: the transactional theory of the literacy work.* Carbondale, IL: Southern Illinois Press.

Routman, R. 1988. *Transitions: From literature to literacy.* Portsmouth, NH: Heinemann.

Smith, F. 1985. *Reading without nonsense.* New York: Teachers College Press.

———. 1988. *Joining the literacy club.* Portsmouth, NH: Heinemann.

Smith, F., E. Brooks, K. S. Goodman, and R. Meredith. 1970. *Language and thinking in the elementary school.* New York: Holt, Rinehart & Winston.

Stephens, D. 1987. Empowering learning: Research as practical theory. *English Education* 19: 220–28.

———. 1989. Three strategies that make a difference. In How we might begin: Insights from research and practice, ed. J. Harste and D. Stephens. Typescript.

Stephens, D., J. Story, K. O'Neill, J. Toomes, R. Huntsman, and V. Watson. 1990. We call it good teaching. In *Portraits of whole language classrooms*, ed. H. Mills and D. Whitin. Portsmouth, NH: Heinemann.

Story, J. 1988. Teaching as response. Typescript.

Strickland, D. 1988. The teacher as researcher: Toward the extended professional. *Language Arts* 65 (8): 754–64.

Temple, C., R. Nathan, and N. Burris. 1982. *The beginning of writing.* Boston: Allyn & Bacon.

Twain, M. 1884. *The adventures of Huckleberry Finn.* New York: Harper.

Voss, M. 1988. "Make way for applesauce": The literate world of a three-year-old. *Language Arts* 65: 272–78.

Watson, D. 1985. Watching and listening to children read. In Jagger and Smith-Burke 1985, 115–28.

Weaver, C. 1988. *Reading process and practice: From sociolinguistics to whole language.* Portsmouth, NH: Heinemann.

Wells, G. 1986. *The meaning makers.* Portsmouth, NH: Heinemann.

Wright Group. 1987. *Story box in the classroom.* Videotape.